Cambridge Elements ≡

Elements in Publishing and Book Culture
edited by
Samantha Rayner
University College London
Leah Tether
University of Bristol

CHINA'S EBOOK EVOLUTION

Disruptive Models and Emerging Book Cultures

Xiang Ren
The University of Sydney

CAMBRIDGE
UNIVERSITY PRESS

CAMBRIDGE
UNIVERSITY PRESS

Shaftesbury Road, Cambridge CB2 8EA, United Kingdom

One Liberty Plaza, 20th Floor, New York, NY 10006, USA

477 Williamstown Road, Port Melbourne, VIC 3207, Australia

314–321, 3rd Floor, Plot 3, Splendor Forum, Jasola District Centre,
New Delhi – 110025, India

103 Penang Road, #05–06/07, Visioncrest Commercial, Singapore 238467

Cambridge University Press is part of Cambridge University Press & Assessment,
a department of the University of Cambridge.

We share the University's mission to contribute to society through the pursuit of
education, learning and research at the highest international levels of excellence.

www.cambridge.org
Information on this title: www.cambridge.org/9781009464840

DOI: 10.1017/9781009464864

First published 2024

A catalogue record for this publication is available from the British Library.

ISBN 978-1-009-46484-0 Paperback
ISSN 2514-8524 (online)
ISSN 2514-8516 (print)

China's eBook Evolution

Disruptive Models and Emerging Book Cultures

Elements in Publishing and Book Culture

DOI: 10.1017/9781009464864

First published online: May 2024

Xiang Ren

The University of Sydney

Author for correspondence: Xiang Ren, x.ren@sydney.edu.au

ABSTRACT: This Element explores the changing landscape of eBook businesses and cultures in China in the past two decades and examines how disruptive innovation and platform economy have transformed one of the world's largest book markets. Through an evolutionary perspective, this Element documents and analyses the emergence, growth, and refinement of disruptive models in three areas of trade publishing, including free eBook developments, digital self-publishing, and platformed social reading. It offers a critical account of the complex interplay between emerging technologies, business innovations, and book cultures and conceptualises China's eBook evolution as both a part of global digital publishing transformation in the platform age and an embodiment of local dynamics in a transitional society. This Element is essential for scholars, students, publishers, and the interested publics to understand China's digital publishing innovations and their global implications.

KEYWORDS: digital publishing, China, reading, digital cultures, business model

ISBNs: 9781009464840 (PB), 9781009464864 (OC)

ISSNs: 2514-8524 (online), 2514-8516 (print)

Contents

1 Introduction

On 30 June 2023, Amazon ceased the operations of its Kindle eBook Store in China, bringing an end to its ten-year venture in one of the world's largest book markets. This move did not come as a surprise, as Amazon had announced the withdrawal a year ago, after the closure of its online bookstore and e-commerce site in China. The 'stringent censorship rules and a fiercely competitive home-grown technology ecosystem' were regarded as key reasons for the retreat (Strumpf, 2022). Inside China's book world, the withdrawal reignited a debate on the future of eBooks. While readers and publishers are concerned about the loss of Kindle as a reliable source of eBook content and revenue, some pointed out that the eBook models represented by Kindle might be outdated, as Amazon has been struggling to compete with local eBook vendors when it comes to identifying and fulfilling the changing demands of digital reading in a vast and dynamic market like China (Meng, 2022).

The Kindle revolution, driven by Amazon's robust digital ecosystem, including Kindle devices, online bookstores, Kindle Direct Publishing (KDP), Audible, and Kindle Unlimited, has been a disruptive force to legacy publishing businesses across the world (Konoval, 2015). Kindle's arrival in China in 2013 was perceived as a 'catfish' that would stir up the market by bringing in established digital business models, setting a high industrial standard, and educating consumers' e-reading awareness (Lei, 2013). Indeed, Kindle did enjoy a long honeymoon with substantial commercial success in China, which became the company's largest market outside the United States in 2017 (Goh, 2022). However, the subsequent years marked a decline in Kindle's fortunes in China, partially due to the lack of significant innovations in its approach to eBooks and digital reading.

Based on specialist eReader hardware, Amazon Kindle offers a standardised eBook experience and monotonous reader interface, locked in a closed ecosystem with limited functionality and interoperability (Kreutzmann-Gallasch & Schroff, 2022). However, China's eBook market has been evolving rapidly, fuelled by local innovations that offer more competitive, functional, and affordable eBook products and services (Yuan & Hu, 2022). For instance, Chinese e-ink device manufacturers like Onyx, BigMe, and Hanvon have long been developing a range of screen sizes from 4 to 13.3 inches to meet diverse market demands and compete with the Kindle eReader. These devices run the latest Android operating systems, boosted with advanced tech specifications, allowing users to access almost all mainstream eBook platforms in one device, including Kindle, Kobo, iReader, Duokan, and WeChat Read, as well as install millions of Android apps. Digital reading functions have also been further optimised for PDFs, note-taking, and knowledge management to tailor the needs of educational and professional users. Compared with local competitors, it is unsurprising that Chinese consumers find Kindle eReader less useful (Qin, 2022). Thus, they humorously call it a makeshift lid, useful only for covering a cup of boiling instant noodles.

The more profound challenge faced by Amazon Kindle in China lies in business models. The Chinese internet giants like Tencent and ByteDance, based on super apps like WeChat and Douyin (Chinese version of TikTok), are aggressively expanding into digital reading markets, leveraging their large user bases, infrastructural capabilities, and integrated ecosystems to provide new opportunities for authors and create more captivating experiences for readers (Jia et al., 2022; Su, 2023). Local digital publishing companies owned by or affiliated with big tech firms can also diversify their revenue streams through online advertising, e-commerce, and cross-subsidisation (Zhang et al., 2021). This allows them to offer inexpensive, or even free, eBook services. By contrast, Amazon's global dominance, based on its monopolist platform ecosystem, does not translate into advantages in China's locally controlled internet ecosystem. As a result, the disadvantage of Kindle's dated eBook model, with 'technological limitations and mundane aesthetics' (Loewenstein, 2014), is being amplified.

Factors like government censorship and the monopoly of local platforms have undoubtedly played a role in Kindle's struggles in China. China's increasing techno-nationalism in the Xi Jinping era also contributes to Amazon's withdrawal, stemming from both government favouritism towards domestic companies and shifting consumer attitudes against international brands (Luo, 2022). However, Kindle's experience underscores an important issue in the globalisation of book publishing: the prevailing 'one-size-fits-all' approach adopted by Western publishing companies may fail to grasp the evolutionary complexities of emerging markets like China. The challenge of Amazon Kindle is a snapshot of the disparity between the Western and

Chinese digital publishing landscapes, which has not been fully recognised and understood in global publishing communities, making it difficult to engage with the vast eBook market there.

I write this Element with an initial motivation to demystify the digital publishing system in China, which, while too big to ignore, can be complicated for outsiders to understand, given its differences and rapid changes. However, I do not simply portray China as a mysterious landscape and isolated 'Other', focusing solely on how different it could be. Rather, I perceive China's eBook evolution as an important, complex, yet underappreciated arena for digital publishing innovation, underpinned by a parallel pathway for digital transformation but with significant interconnections with the global publishing world.

In doing so, this Element surfaces important lessons from China's dynamic eBook evolution that may offer insights for global publishing communities, as well as opportunities for collaboration and engagement. Specifically, it focuses on three areas in trade book publishing where disruptive digital models thrive, including free eBooks, platformed self-publishing, and social reading. The disruptive models examined in this work, some of which may initially appear to mirror their Western counterparts, exhibit unique business practices and evolutionary trajectories in China, characterised by a myriad of indigenous and adaptive innovations and emerging book cultures. While examining China's eBook evolution driven by disruptive models over the past two decades or so, this Element highlights these developments as illustrations of China's digital publishing transformation and further contextualises the transformative changes into both China's social transitions and global publishing evolution, with a hope to broaden and diversify our understanding on publishing futures.

1.1 China's eBook Landscape

By any measure, China is one of the world's largest markets for eBook and digital publishing. In China's policy and industry settings, the term 'digital publishing' is defined in its broadest sense, encompassing a wide range of digital content industries, ranging from online advertising to mobile publishing, gaming, eLearning, and digital music, with a total revenue of RMB 1,276 billion (USD 175 billion) in 2021, whereas conventional eBook business only generated RMB 6.6 billion (USD 0.82 billion) (Statista, 2021). Although this Element does not examine the entire digital publishing landscape in China, it defines eBook developments based on this broad conceptualisation, which probably differs from the industrial perception of eBooks in the Western context, as typically 'another format in which publishers could package books and deliver them to consumers' (Thompson, 2021:579). In other words, this Element moves beyond the publisher-controlled conventional eBook domain and instead explores various eBook dynamics ranging from mobile publishing to platformed webnovels (also known as online literature in China), WeChat social reading, and BookTok on Douyin, which better reflect the multifaceted yet innovative developments of eBooks in China. Before delving into these practices, it is necessary to introduce the Chinese context of eBooks and digital publishing, including the business environment, regulatory frameworks, and reading publics.

1.1.1 The Power Dynamics between Publishers and Platforms
The global evolution of digital publishing can be marked by a power struggle between traditional publishers and digital platforms (Rashidian et al., 2019). In China, legacy publishers have also faced challenges negotiating with both tech giants and emerging start-ups from a comparatively weaker position in the digital ecosystem. When the digital publishing revolution started in the late 1990s, the Chinese print publishing industry was less modernised and advanced than its Western counterparts, and most publishers were relatively small in scale (Tian & Martin, 2013). Despite their privileged position due to government control over market entry, few Chinese publishers had the necessary technological, economic, and human resources to develop a viable digital publishing business. Publishers' digital strategies were also largely confined to traditional business logic, as many saw eBooks as experimental and supplementary tools to promote physical books while being concerned about the threat they posed to print sales (Li, 2023). Some publishing houses, like their counterparts in other markets, resisted digital transformation by refusing to release digital versions of their new and bestselling titles, pricing their eBooks higher than print versions, and adding complicated digital right protections, which, however, all undermined digital reading experience (Ren, 2022).

This provided opportunity for digital disruptors to thrive by entering previously restricted publishing domains and disrupting legacy publishing models. The combination of self-publishing, non-exclusive licensing and digital piracy offered Chinese emerging eBook vendors sufficient content resources to maintain the growth of their businesses in the early stage. Platformed webnovels, as a unique development of digital self-publishing, which will be discussed in Chapter 3 in detail, provided millions of online fiction stories, allowing experimental models of authoring, editing, publishing, and monetising, which became a major content supplier for disruptive eBook initiatives. Meanwhile, as book contracts signed in the print age normally excluded eBook editions in China, the market for eBook copyright became chaotic, where authors, publishers, and agencies all claimed their legal rights. This complicated copyright protection in the eBook field, where rampant digital piracy and copyright infringement – ranging from peer sharing to pirated eBook portals – had already been a big threat to traditional publishers. Around 2011, for instance, many Chinese writers and publishers filed lawsuits against Baidu Wenku, an online library and document-sharing platform operated by Baidu, for the unauthorised sharing and republishing of digital publications. This legal action was taken due to Baidu's alleged substantial economic gains through copyright infringement, particularly allowing millions of users to upload and share copyrighted works without permission (Cao, 2012). In short, as regulations lagged behind innovations in the early years of eBook evolution in China, the field was largely the Wide West, where disruptors had more opportunities and resources than traditional publishers.

Since 2010, Chinese state-owned publishing houses have undergone significant corporate restructuring, including mergers, acquisitions, and financing on the stock market. This has enabled them to adopt modern business practices and leverage capital markets to fund expansion and innovation (Chen, 2011). Chinese publishing groups gradually became competitive with large-scale business operations. In 2022, three Chinese publishing groups were listed among the world's top fifty in *Publishers Weekly*'s annual global ranking (Milliot, 2022). Alongside government-backed and state-owned publishing groups, China also has a thriving private book publishing sector with leading players like Motie, New Classic, and Cheers in major areas of trade books. In the past decade or so, Chinese publishers have evolved with greater economic and technological capabilities to drive digital innovation and upgrading, along with the encouragement policy and financial support from the Chinese government. The industrial transformation has concluded the era of radical disruptions but opened a new stage of convergence between traditional publishers and internet platforms, encompassing both the digitisation of print book businesses and the formalisation of born-digital disruptions.

However, this has not fundamentally altered the power dynamic between publishers and platforms for two reasons. Firstly, eBook sales still represent a relatively small portion of publishers' revenue, only up to 10 per cent on average (Cui, 2022; Open Book, 2023). As a result, publishers still rely on print book markets for profitability and financial sustainability, particularly educational books, paperback bestsellers, and children's books, being reluctant to make substantial investments in eBook innovations. The second reason is the dominance of technology giants and their digital content ecosystem, as will be discussed in detail in this Element. For instance, Tencent launched WeChat Read, a top social reading app based on the WeChat ecosystem, and owns the largest webnovel company, Yuwen Group (internationally known as China Literature). Likewise, ByteDance (also known as Douyin Group in China) offers digital infrastructures for BookTok and book livestreaming e-commerce in China, directly contributing to nearly 20 per cent of book sales in 2022 (Open Book, 2023), in addition to ad-supported free eBook platforms. As such, while publishing groups grow rapidly, the disruptive eBook models based on tech giants' platform ecosystems are further revolutionising the eBook business, making platforms still powerful in the digital transformation of book publishing in China.

1.1.2 The Regulatory 'Special Zone' of Digital Publishing

While China's stringent regulation and censorship of publishing is globally acknowledged, the government's substantial role in fostering and directing the industrial transformation (or 'digital upgrading' in the policy term) receives less attention. It is incontestable that China's sophisticated and restrictive system of publishing control and censorship, as outlined by Freedom House (Einarsson et al., 2023), extends into the digital domain.

In the eBook sector, the government maintains rigorous control over market entry, mandating businesses to register with appropriate regulatory bodies to operate, while foreign firms must undergo a special approval process (Wang, 2014). Additionally, authors on prominent platforms such as webnovels are required to complete real name verification, which also gradually applies to users wishing to post comments in various discussions (Ren, 2020).

On the other hand, when it comes to politically non-sensitive content, digital publishing in China operates within a relatively more lenient regulatory environment than its print counterpart, resulting in a regulatory 'special zone' in practice. If the early Wild West stage of eBook evolution could be attributed largely to lagging regulatory responses to new disruptive technologies, the 'special zone' after the mid-2010s came more from the government's strategic intention of encouraging and facilitating digital upgrading of the traditional publishing sector, as an integral part of China's digital creative economy (Wang et al., 2019).

Unlike in European countries, where eBook regulations often strive to protect legacy publishers from digital disruptions (Heyman, 2015), the Chinese government is eager to leverage digital innovation to reform and upgrade its traditional publishing system and catch up with the developed countries. As early as 2010, the General Administration of Press and Publication (2010) had set a clear yet ambitious goal: by 2020, all state-owned publishing houses should have essentially completed their digital transformation, achieving a world-leading level of digital publishing innovation. Accordingly, the Chinese government's policy on eBooks and digital publishing endeavours to facilitate the digital upgrading of traditional publishers and encourage collaborations between publishers and internet companies under the government-backed agendas of 'Internet plus publishing' and digital creative economy (Flew et al., 2019). In addition to advocacy and policy encouragement, the Chinese government has also directly invested in both national-level digital publishing infrastructure projects and publisher-led digital initiatives, such as national labs, book digitisation projects, the development of industry standards, and national big data centres.

As already discussed, China employs a broad definition of digital publishing, which helps legitimise content censorship across all emerging digital content industries. However, it also signifies an official and increasingly mainstream understanding of digital publishing in China as a broad transmedia, cross-sector, and inter-platform system rather than merely digitised print publishing. From a policy perspective, it fosters industry convergence by removing regulatory restrictions, allowing internet platforms to operate in the publishing industry and even integrate eBooks into their ecosystems. On the other hand, platforms' rapid expansion and cross-sector integration in digital publishing impose regulatory challenges, particularly from blurred and ill-defined boundaries between the oversight jurisdictions of different government institutions. The lack of effective regulatory division and coordination has thus negatively impacted the efficacy of regulation (Huang & Hao, 2014). As such, the Chinese platform companies have benefited from a more relaxed regulatory environment than their Western counterparts, with less regulatory pressure on issues like industrial concentration, cross-media ownership, and the protection of user rights and privacy, which help sustain rapid economic growth and fast-paced innovations in eBooks and digital publishing sectors.

The overall regulatory environment in China significantly changed after the second term of Xi Jinping in 2017, as the focus started shifting from growth and innovation to the control of platform power. The so-called tech clash in China, as put by Xi Jinping himself, aims to 'prevent the irrational expansion of capital' and address the problem of 'barbarous growth' in the internet industry (Bartholomeusz, 2022). The improvement of regulatory coordination and efficacy appears in various areas, from anti-trust to content censorship to digital copyright protection, mandating platforms to bear more responsibilities and explicitly express political loyalty (Wu, 2022). The broad regulatory change in digital platforms unavoidably influenced the eBook sector, demonstrated by the changes ranging from enhanced enforcement of copyright protection and censorship to fairer distribution of economic benefits between self-published authors and webnovel platforms (Global Times, 2020). This serves as a reminder that, despite comparable regulatory dynamics propelling innovations, digital publishing regulation in China remains a statist, top-down approach under strong government influence, distinguishing it from regulatory practices in the Western context.

1.1.3 Digital Reading Publics

It may be surprising to some that the purchasing rate of eBooks in China surpasses that of the US. In 2021, 26.1 per cent of China's population purchased eBooks, compared to 23.4 per cent in the US, though Chinese readers still dramatically lag in average spending on eBooks and overall print book purchases (Richter, 2022; Statista, n.d.). This trend indicates China's expansive yet under-explored digital reading market that affords digital publishing an unprecedented opportunity to grow and evolve, particularly through engaging with new digital reading publics.

Early in the digital publishing revolution, surveys showed a gradual decline in China's print book reading population that read at least once a month, dropping from 60 per cent in 1999 to 48.7 per cent in 2005 (Hao et al., 2008). The rise of eBooks expanded China's reading population through digital innovations and, interestingly, by attracting those who did not read books in the print age. The rapid expansion of the eBook business from 2005 to 2015 coincided with the burgeoning popularisation of mobile internet and smartphones across China (Chen, 2011), enabling those who had not even used desktop computers before to access the digital world conveniently. During that period, digital reading experienced two-digit fast growth (Mei, 2023), as a result of which, in 2015, according to the twelfth annual national reading survey conducted by the China Publication and Press Research Institute, the rate of digital reading surpassed that of print reading for the first time (Xie, 2015). The catalyst driving the eBook growth was largely the previously marginalised demographics, in particular, those with low levels of education and low socio-economic status (Ren, 2016).

As such, the digital revolution in China was a process of democratising books and reading, with profound implications of knowledge equity and social justice, even comparable to the paperback revolution in the West. Meanwhile, the new reading publics inevitably created a shift in literary demand, contrasting with the previous elitist reading culture, which practically led to the prevalence of self-published web-novels and cheap or free eBook models in the 2010s. Unsurprisingly, the 'barbaric growth' of digital reading attracted criticisms from China's official media outlets, citing problems like the proliferation of low-quality texts, pornography and violence, fragmented and shallow reading forms, and rampant piracy and plagiarism (Dong & Wu, 2017).

Parallel to the democratising process featured by emerging digital reading publics, China's print reading population is changing their reading habits, consuming quality eBooks formally published by traditional publishers. The launch of Amazon's Kindle to the Chinese market in 2013 was a landmark event boosting the digital reading market of the educated urban middle class, making Kindle eReader one of the most trendy consumer commodities at that time (Yuan & Hu, 2022). The evolution of China's internet ecosystem led by tech giants like BAT, particularly their digital transaction and payment systems, based on Alipay and WeChat Pay, has further propelled the digital transformation of public reading, accelerating the growth of paying users. In 2020, before the pandemic, the total number of digital readers in China rose to 494 million, who consumed an average of 9.1 eBooks that year in both free and paid platforms, compared to only 6.2 print books (CADPA, 2021). Further indicative of this trend, China's total digital readership base had expanded to 530 million in 2022 (Mei, 2023).

Although the statistics demonstrate the massive scale of eBook and digital reading businesses across China, traditional publishers have not reaped comparable revenues or economic gains. This disconnect is attributable to the prevalence of free eBook services and the low average pricing of books and eBooks in the Chinese market, as well as ascendant disruptive forces outside the traditional publishing domain. As will be further explored in this Element, internet giants like Tencent and ByteDance nowadays dominate important areas like webnovels, mobile reading, and social reading, leveraging their status to restructure the digital publishing value chain and siphoning profits once flowing to traditional publishers. The resultant industrial structure of eBook publishing in China, with its complex interplay between publishers, platforms, and digital reading publics, thus cultivates a unique confluence of eBook cultures and socio-economic transitions.

1.2 An Evolutionary Approach

As already discussed in Chapter 1.1, China has a multifaceted and evolving eBook landscape, characterised by the changing power dynamics between publishers and platforms, the government-backed digital upgrading strategy, and the emergence of digital reading publics, which encompasses a broad spectrum of economic, cultural, and political issues previously under-explored in publishing research. While publishing, researchers have long been interested in the collision between 'the oldest of our media industries' and 'the great technological revolution of our time' (Thompson, 2021:17); they tend to understand the evolutionary nature of digital publishing based on a perceived distinction between the 'disruptive' and the 'traditional' (Ren, 2022). Accordingly, the research agenda within the field usually focuses on how the traditional publishing community (publishers and authors in particular) copes with the disruptive forces and models, such as digital self-publishing, Amazon platform, BookTok, and Open AI (Gilbert, 2015; Ross, 2016; Driscoll et al., 2018; Bhaskar, 2020; Dezuanni et al., 2022).

In this Element, while I share the view that there is a publishing community that should benefit from digital innovation, I explore eBook evolution more from the perspectives of the disruptors and their engagement with the reading and writing publics. In doing so, I regard the disruptive models and transformative changes as part of an ongoing evolution of book publishing at large and as part of the emerging digital platform ecosystem instead of something that distinguishes and thus separates the traditional and digital publishing sectors. This approach starts with Clayton Christensen's original idea of disruptive innovation, referring to the innovations that make products and services more accessible and affordable to a larger population (Christensen et al., 2018). China's digital publishing innovation, while rarely a genuine breakthrough, presents uniquely valuable experiments with such disruptive ideas at a vast scale. Contrasting to China's restricted, costly, and censored print publishing system, internet companies, start-ups, and even entrepreneurial individuals harness digital dynamics to cater to previously underserved publics or increase public access to digital realms of reading and writing. In this Element, I examine various such cases whose value proposition could be eventually understood as accessibility and affordability. In addition to critical analysis of the evolutionary trajectory of disruptive initiatives that grow and displace established models, I also link the industrial disruption with book cultures and social changes, in particular, the democratising process of writing and reading in China. As such, I further examine the interplay between disruptive innovations and the social, cultural, and political value of disruptive practices of eBooks and how they may function as a progressive and liberalising force in a transitional society and an authoritarian regime like China.

However, the evolutionary approach adopted by this Element does not solely build upon digital optimism or Californian Ideology (Hepp et al., 2023). Rather, by examining the evolution of eBooks in the past twenty years or so, the approach grounds disruption and transformation historically and explores the complex and changing tensions associated with different evolutionary stages: the pioneering yet chaotic years from the late 1990s to early 2010s featuring various radical disruptions and progressive innovations, the profound processes of platformisation and convergence in the decade after, and the development of digital publishing platform ecosystems increasingly dominated by tech giants and controlled by the Party-State. Drawing on critical political economy and platform studies (Mansell & Steinmueller, 2020; Flew, 2021; Nielsen & Sarah, 2022), I employ a twofold analytical framework. On the one hand, I map the business dynamics and opportunities that emerged from the integration of eBooks and online advertising, e-commerce, influencer economy, and transmedia entertainment in tech giants' platform ecosystems and examine the sustainability of digital publishing in an extended value chain. On the other hand, I critically explore the power dynamics between publishers, platforms, regulators, digital intermediaries, and the writing and reading publics, as well as the issues like digital labour (Scholz, 2012), infrastructural intermediation (Hutchinson, 2023), and platform governance (Van Dijck et al., 2023). Accordingly, I interrogate the multiple roles of platforms in eBook evolution as a disruptor to legacy publishing, a monopolist of digital resources, an infrastructural intermediary of digital content, and a tech-powered mechanism for censorship in China, which will shed new light on digital publishing research in the age of platform economy.

This Element draws on my ongoing research in the business and cultures of China's digital publishing and my involvement with the industry as a former publisher from the late 1990s to the early 2010s. Based on multiple case studies, the major data sources for this work include (1) corporate releases, annual reports, and industry statistics published by major eBook vendors, internet companies, traditional publishers, and governmental and research institutes; (2) ethnographic data, including observational notes on eBook platforms, archived public social media posts, and private communications; and (3) trade press publications from reputable media outlets across the past twenty years, including the reports and commentaries on major eBook developments and public interviews with stakeholders in the different historical contexts.

Drawing on China's eBook evolution, I hope this Element contributes to the global discourse on digital publishing futures, in particular, the impact of ongoing digital dynamics (e.g., convergence and platform capitalism) and next-gen disruptive technologies (e.g., blockchain and generative AI) on the business practices, cultures, and values of book publishing. There are already valuable works that endeavour to re-conceptualise books (Phillips & Kovač, 2022) or redefine publishers' roles as curators (Bhaskar, 2016) or knowledge service providers (Thompson, 2021) in a digital context. This Element, while inspired by these works, aims to conceptualise an ongoing process of co-evolution between the established and emerging forces, where constant disruption is the new normal. Instead of merely advising traditional publishers on surviving the digital disruption or battling against disruptors, the ambition of this work is to revisit some of the crucial questions on publishing through an evolutionary perspective, such as the longevity of publishing business models, the resilience of book publishing, the autonomy of writers and creators, and the protection of communal or public interests.

1.3 Chapter Outline

This Element comprises five chapters. The introduction chapter briefly outlines the background, purpose, and approach of the work and offers an overview of China's digital publishing context. Chapters 2–4 are three case study chapters, each focusing on one area of disruptive eBook developments. Chapter 2 embarks on free eBook developments in the past decades in China and examines several waves of disruptive innovations that cater to a market of price-sensitive readers and the new reading publics through affordable and accessible eBooks. It explores how the free eBook model is being re-imagined beyond the traditional book business and shaped by the changing publishing economy in the platform age, which sheds new light on the global debates of 'free versus paid' in digital content industries and knowledge equity in a digital society.

Chapter 3 delves into the area of platformed digital self-publishing with a refreshed and evolving perspective on the labour and power of webnovels, drawing on a chronological mapping of Chinese webnovel evolution from the 1990s to the present, traversing from grassroots disruptions to platformisation to digital entertainment ecosystem. It explores the multifaceted roles of networked writing publics as participatory fan-creators, content entrepreneurs, and cheap labourers in the digital publishing economy, fuelling the disruptive innovations with original content and creative labour, and further discusses the implications for the next wave of disruption driven by generative AI.

Chapter 4 shifts focus to digital reading publics and social reading evolution. However, instead of assuming a distributed and participatory framework of social reading, it critically inquiries into the role of platforms in reshaping social reading in China, ranging from eBook portals to social media giants like WeChat, QQ and Douyin (TikTok). In doing so, this chapter maps the evolving practices of platform-mediated social reading, in particular, the integration between digital reading and social media ecosystems in China, which offers a new context to analyse the economic value of reading and the power dynamics between readers, publishers, and super apps.

Chapter 5 concludes this Element by summarising the key features of China's eBook evolution and further discussing their implications in a global digital context, where publishing communities across the world grapple with the next generation of disruptive technologies and uncertain economic environments. For this, China is both a global powerhouse of digital publishing business and an inspiring experimental playground for new ideas.

2 Free eBooks in a Changing Publishing Economy

2.1 Do eBooks Want to Be Free?

In April 2013, Dangdang, one of China's largest online bookstores and e-commerce platforms, launched a three-day promotion where users could download almost all its eBooks for free. This sudden giveaway campaign was perhaps one of the most controversial experiments in China's eBook history and, unsurprisingly, received considerable backlash from publishers and authors. They regarded it as a significant infringement of copyright and demanded the removal of their titles from the platform (Wright, 2013). Adding to the controversy was Dangdang's decision to proceed with the campaign even without obtaining prior consent from its publishing partners, as publishers would receive no revenues under the profit-sharing agreement based on actual sales (Liu, 2013).

In defence of their bold move, Dangdang claimed that the initiative aimed to foster public reading of copyrighted eBooks and combat rampant piracy. According to the statistics from Dangdang, the campaign led to a significant increase in eBook downloads, rising to several hundred times the usual volume, which highlighted the vast market potential of digital reading in China at a time when the industry was experiencing stagnant growth with an uncertain future (Meng, 2012). However, the experiment sparked much anger among Chinese publishers. While very few publishers eventually pursued legal action against Dangdang due to its dominant position as a distribution channel for physical books, many publicly expressed their resentment (Liu, 2013). They believed such promotion, instead of cultivating public digital reading, would devalue eBooks in the market and undermine the ongoing effort to convert Chinese readers into eBook purchasers (Wright, 2013). To some, Dangdang's campaign was nothing but a calculated attempt to enhance the popularity and capacity of its e-commerce platform at the expense of the book publishing industry (Ma, 2013).

Looking through the perspective of today's platform age, the event serves as a powerful reminder of the profound tension between publishers and authors who produce content and platforms that mediate and profit from it in ways that often escape the control of the rightful owners and diverge from their business logic and principles (Thompson, 2021). Central to such tension is the competition and co-evolution between free and paid content models in the digital age. While offering eBooks for free to readers showcases undeniable commercial potential, especially when supported by alternative financial channels in the expansive platform economy, the interests, rights, and financial sustainability of publishers and authors are primarily anchored in the conventional reader-pay paradigm of the book business.

In the evolving landscape of the digital publishing economy, how can the free eBook model be re-imagined beyond the traditional book business? Is it possible to re-balance the power between platforms and publishers in the value chain of free eBooks? Regarding the social and cultural implications, how do free eBooks expand the digital reading sphere and transform book cultures?

The disruptive innovation of free eBooks in China offers a valuable case to address these questions. Dangdang's bold experiment is a snapshot of China's continuing eBook developments to cater to a market of price-sensitive readers reluctant to pay for digital content. Thus, the idea of free eBooks constantly gained renewed attention in China's eBook evolution, aligned with different dynamics: from hardware-sponsored eBook giveaways to complimentary eBook subscriptions bundled with mobile phone plans, from ad-supported mobile reading apps to the unlimited reading cards awarded to WeChat users. Waves of free eBook disruptions are transforming China's digital publishing economy. Instead of relying merely on eBook sales, mainstream eBook vendors are gradually adopting hybrid models with a significant component of free eBook offerings, which tend to diversify and complicate revenue streams for eBook business and broadly redefine the book publishing economy. This chapter reviews the evolutionary developments of China's free eBook models and examines their innovations and impact on the book publishing business. In doing so, it sheds new light on the 'free versus paid' debate across content industries in an evolving publishing economy and explores alternative eBook models for sustainability and knowledge equity.

2.2 The Struggles of Paid eBook Business

2.2.1 Where Are the Paying Readers?

The business logic of the book publishing industry, relatively unchanged since the Gutenberg age, assumes that readers pay for content they find useful, valuable, or entertaining. The book authors' and publishers' economic and social value is typically monetised and measured through reader payments (or the copies sold). In other words, unlike newspapers or magazines, readers, instead of advertisers, are the primary master for whom the book business creates value. As for those who could not afford books, public libraries, charities, discounted bookstores, or second-hand markets provided cheaper access to books in the print age. In the digital age, the negligible cost of digital reproduction has made free eBooks not only feasible but also appealing to the public, who gain free access to eBooks through the Gutenberg project, open access book portals like AOPEN, and pirated eBook sites like Z-library.

The conventional paid eBook model has grappled with challenges in China due to weak copyright enforcement and rampant eBook piracy. It was estimated that there were 14,000 eBook piracy portals or shadow libraries available in China (Chi, 2013), which disincentivised internet users from paying for eBooks. Unsurprisingly, there is a significant difference in the average amount spent on eBooks by users in China compared to those in the US. In 2017, Chinese users spent only USD 2.13 purchasing eBooks, and the amount increased to USD 3.89 in 2022. In comparison, US users spent USD 18.25 in 2017 and USD 22.63 in 2022 (Statista, n.d.). This disparity highlights the challenges faced by publishers in China, who found it difficult to establish sustainable business models to generate revenues when they ventured into the eBook market (Tian & Martin, 2013). Facing the digital revolution, publishers in China encountered a quandary that gave rise to an industry saying: while resistance to digital innovation spells eventual obsolescence, embracing eBooks would risk losing all commercial interests immediately (Ren, 2016).

In the early 2010s, major eBook vendors that relied on paid models faced significant challenges. For instance, Fanshu, the eBook portal established by

China's dominant publishing technology company, Founder, recorded a meagre revenue of RMB 1.14 million (USD 175,000) against losses of over RMB 20 million (USD 3.1 million) in 2010 (Ren, 2019). Apart from users' reluctance to pay, low revenue also resulted from poor eBook experiences, including outdated titles, difficulty in navigating content, limited functionality, and unnecessarily complicated DRM protections (Myrberg, 2017). China's internet start-ups like Duokan endeavoured to address these problems by optimising digital content, user interface, and reading functionality, with an ambition of surpassing the pleasure of print reading (Xu, 2013; Wang, 2014). However, despite a series of innovations improving user experience in their eBook stores across Kindle, iOS, and Android platforms, only 350,000 of Duokan's 25 million registered users paid for an eBook in 2013 (Zhang, 2014).

This reflects the conundrum almost all Chinese eBook vendors faced in the early 2010s. While new technologies and internet cultures could progressively transform perceptions and expectations of digital reading, monetising such investments was still confined within the conventional paid eBook model. Such a traditional model encountered significant challenges in the Chinese market due to the prevailing reading habits of free content and a lack of market readiness for high-quality paid eBooks. Consequently, innovators were forced to explore alternative models, offering free or inexpensive content while seeking diverse revenue sources.

2.2.2 Subsidised eBooks Models

The leading Chinese eBook companies like iReader, Duokan, and Dangdang, mirroring Western platforms like Amazon and Kobo, have all used freemium and limited free offerings frequently to attract readers and foster reading habits, with a hope of gradually converting free users into paying readers. Meanwhile, the sponsored free eBooks model based on the partnership between eBook vendors and hardware companies also became popular. For instance, Hanvon gifted device buyers with a package of 5,000 copyrighted eBooks around 2010 to promote their pricy e-reading device, which was usually sold as an expensive business gift (Qin, 2010). However, a truly defining moment in the eBook sector was the launch of the China Mobile Reading Base in May 2010, built upon a strategic partnership between the former General Administration of Press and Publication and the state-owned telecommunication corporation China Mobile, which was practically based at China Mobile Zhejiang Company. With the growing popularity of smartphones in China, China Mobile operated a multimedia entertainment ecosystem based on smartphones, where the mobile reading base coexisted with other bases for music, animation, games, and video. As monthly subscription was the standard business model for all these content areas, the Reading Base also adopted it in its eBook business, which, however, was pioneering in the publishing world at that time, even earlier than the similar Kindle Unlimited.

The subscription model possessed an unparalleled price advantage, at only RMB 3 (USD 40 cents) per month in 2011, making it highly affordable to mobile phone users (Zhejiang Mobile, 2011). The Reading Base further combined eBook subscriptions with monthly mobile phone charges, along-side other multimedia content bundles, presenting the eBook subscription as a bonus for recharging phone plans, eliminating the need for direct cash payment. The Base soon attracted 73.4 million active users and made an annual revenue of RMB 1.5 billion (USD 200 million) in 2011 (Wu & Zhang, 2012). To Chinese mobile phone users seeking relaxing, time-fulfilling, and casual reading, such an eBook offering was more attractive than expensive print books. Moreover, this almost complimentary subscription model effectively attracted a unique demographic into digital reading – less educated, low-income individuals and rural immigrants who were not regular print readers (Ren, 2019).

The Chinese born-digital and self-published webnovels, initially published on various online platforms, became one of the major content sources for the Base. Additionally, the Base attempted to attract traditional publishers by suggesting that offering already-published books digitally is like a secondary release, which could boost publishers' income, especially for older titles that may not be profitable to republish in print due to limited demand (Zhejiang Mobile, 2011). By defining mobile publishing as a digital extension of the print book business, and with the endorsement from the National Bureau of Publication and Press, the Base successfully partnered with over 160 content providers in 2012, securing licenses for 350,000 titles from both traditional and online publishers (Wu & Zhang, 2012). To many book publishers and authors, the earnings from the Base doubled the revenues generated from other digital channels. For example, the Writers Publishing House licensed 300 literary works to the Base and earned RMB 2 million (USD 0.27 million) in a year, who then distributed half of this amount as digital royalties to their authors. Interestingly, more than ten authors reported that the revenue received from the Base exceeded their traditional royalties in print (Wu & Zhang, 2012). Undeniably, as a state-owned telecommunication monopolist operating a high-profile eBook initiative, China Mobile had a strategic intention of prioritising user growth over profitability for the initial three years (iFeng, 2010), which thus cross-subsidised its eBook venture, allowing the Base to provide users with nearly free eBooks while still offering attractive commissions to publishers.

In April 2015, the China Mobile Reading Base officially rebranded as Migu Read when their model gradually transitioned to conventional eBook stores due to sustainability concerns and increased market competition, reducing advantages gained from subsidised subscriptions. However, their operation in the Chinese eBook market had a significant impact by offering affordable subscription services, which led to a remarkable increase in digital reading, especially among previously overlooked groups. In the formative years of experimental business models, when most companies targeted elite readers with expensive devices and content services (Wang, 2014), the evolutionary value of the Base was in redirecting eBook innovations to increasing access and affordability for the wider masses, ending the stagnation in China's eBook industry at that stage.

2.3 New Wave of Free eBook Disruption

2.3.1 Ad-Supported Mobile Reading Apps

While Chinese eBook companies struggled to expand their paid user base and achieve profitability in the early 2010s, the industry landscape transformed following several key developments. The digital reading population underwent a marked demographic shift as the young generation raised in China's prosperous decades became the primary customer base, with more willingness to pay for digital content (CADPA, 2021). Developments in electronic payment infrastructures, notably through platforms of WeChat Pay and Ali Pay, streamlined online transactions, making eBook purchases easy and convenient. Concurrently, copyright protection and enforcement markedly increased due to strong industry advocacy and China's economic transition towards an innovation-driven digital economy (Yu, 2021). All these elements led to the growth of conventional paid eBook business in China.

However, the threats and challenges still exist. While major pirated eBook portals like KindleRen were closed, mobile reading apps became a new hotspot for eBook piracy, which offer unauthorised versions of bestselling or long-selling eBooks on iOS and Android devices (M. Li, 2017; Y. Li, 2017), threatening the sustainability of paid eBook models. This underscores the complex challenges in establishing a robust and effective system for digital copyright protection in China. The combination of rapid technological innovation, the vast economic scale of digital piracy, social norms tolerating infringing access to content, and the lower priority of copyright regulation compared to political censorship all contribute to the difficulties in developing such a system (Montgomery & Priest, 2016; Domon et al., 2019). It is thus unsurprising that eBook sales still constitute a relatively small portion of the total revenues in China's digital publishing industry (Cui, 2022), leaving market space for ad-supported or cross-subsidised free eBook innovations.

The new wave of free eBook development took shape in 2018 with the launch of mobile reading apps like Midu, Lianshang, and Feidu. These apps adopted wholly free models, offering free eBooks and relying on online advertising, e-commerce commissions, and platform subsidies financially. Such a model becomes viable because China's digital economy has become more mature and established in the late 2010s. Tech giants such as Tencent, ByteDance, Baidu, Alibaba, and China Mobile have established platform ecosystems with e-commerce, social marketing, and online advertising as pillars, boasting vast economic capacity and scale. According to the 44th CNNIC Report, Chinese people spent an average of twenty-eight hours per week online in 2019, with 9 per cent of that time dedicated to reading webnovels, only slightly lower than the highly valued areas by advertisers like short-form video (11.5 per cent) and long-form video (13.4 per cent)

(CNNIC, 2019). All these factors motivate platform companies to explore the market of free digital reading, whose commercial potential might have been undervalued and underexplored.

In May 2018, Qu Toutiao, a mobile technology company, launched a free reading app called Midu Novel. As of December of the same year, the app had attracted 93.8 million monthly active users, including 30.9 million daily active users who spent sixty-three minutes reading free novels on the platform, ranking it as the third most popular digital reading app in China (Qutoutiao Inc., 2019). In the year after, Midu Novel experienced a staggering 286 per cent further growth in monthly active users (Chen, 2022). In 2019, ByteDance entered the free eBook market through its subsidiary, Tomato Novel, with the slogan 'Read all free good books here'. Within the first year, the platform experienced an impressive 276.9 per cent growth in monthly active users (Q Li, 2021), similar to Midu Novel's rapid growth. In April 2020, ByteDance created a dedicated channel for Tomato Novel on its popular online news portal Toutiao, aiming to direct vast existing user traffic towards the new free eBook app. This move also exemplified the Chinese tech giant's strategy of building an integrated transmedia superstructure of digital content and advertising across digital reading, social media, and short videos to foster stickier user experiences and exert greater influence in China's digital economy (Ding, 2021).

The rapid growth of Tomato Novel and Midu Novel indicates a substantial market appetite for free eBooks in China. The frequent interruption of advertisements would undeniably compromise and even undermine the reading experience, especially for elite readers and younger users with less price sensitivity. However, China still has a large low-income population willing to tolerate ad interruptions within the eBook pages in exchange for complimentary content. Like the developments of China Mobile Reading Base, free mobile reading apps like Tomato Novel and Midu Novel expanded by penetrating untapped markets, and this time, older people were a noticeable driver of growth (Deng, 2019; Q. Li 2021; Y. Li, 2021). As the content of these free eBook apps is overwhelmingly webnovels and popular literature, their entertaining nature aligns with the preferences of older internet users who have ample time to kill and often have a higher tolerance for ad interruptions. To retain older users, apps like Tomato Novel even implemented a micropayment reward system that compensates users with a few cents for every hour spent reading on the app (Su, 2022).

Apart from retaining readers, free eBook apps also require original content, particularly captivating webnovels. Therefore, it is crucial to attract and retain online writers who, however, often view the free model as a threat to their creative careers and a devaluation of literary work (Li, 2021). Xie Sipeng, the chief editor of Tomato Novel, thus claimed that as long as the system is transparent and trustworthy, authors can monetise their work and be rewarded under the free model without any issues (Ding, 2021). The platform also developed initiatives like the Starfire and Leading Star Plans to incentivise and reward webnovel writers and nurture content creation. According to their official statistics released in 2023, 1,598 original authors earned over RMB 10,000 (USD 1,367) monthly (Tomato Novel, 2023). Although the income level is not yet enough to attract top-tier writers compared to established paid webnovel platforms, the potential growth opportunities and their appeal to average writers are significant.

2.3.2 Hybrid eBook Models

The emergence of ad-supported free eBook platforms in China presents a significant challenge to traditional publishing models. However, rather than viewing it simply as a threat, those digital publishers and vendors in the paid eBook business also noticed the flourishing digital publishing economy and commercial opportunities brought about by free digital reading. This, however, put them in a complex situation. There is a particular quandary on whether they should venture into the free eBook market for a potentially large readership and advertising revenue, and if so, how to balance the two sharply different approaches to monetising their content.

Yuewen Group (also known as China Literature internationally), a subsidiary of Tencent and the largest company in China's webnovel industry, found itself in such an evolutionary dilemma. The Yuewen Group reported a total revenue of RMB 7.5 billion (USD 1 billion) and 243.9 million monthly active users in 2022 across several leading webnovel platforms it owns, such as Qidian, Hongxiu Tianxiang, and Jinjiang, with paid premium content and intellectual property operations as primary sources (China Literature, 2023). In recent years, the webnovel industry has been prominently impacted by free eBook apps like Tomato Novel and Midu Novel, which offer free webnovels as a major content type. When they surged to the top of mobile reading apps around 2018–2020, the paid users of Yuewen Group decreased from the peak of 11.1 million in 2017 to 9.8 million in 2019 and further to 8.7 million in 2021; concurrently, the ratio of paid users diminished from the peak of 5.8 per cent in 2017 to merely 3.5 per cent in 2021 (Chen, 2022). To cope with the disruptions caused by free models, Yuewen developed its own free eBook platform in addition to the existing freemium system that allows readers to only read the first chapters of a webnovel for free. This move was intended to position Yuewen in direct competition with rival platforms, which, despite increased monthly active users from 2019 to 2022, has not contributed to overall profitability (China Literature, 2023). Moreover, Yuewen's move to free eBook offerings was not well-received within the company, as most of their contracted authors understandably view free online novels as a significant threat to their livelihoods and commercial interests, which led to a massive strike in May 2021, forcing the company to allow authors to choose whether to go for free offerings or not (Sohu, 2020). The authors' view was echoed by academics and commentators in the webnovel field who regarded free eBook developments as a destructive invasion by digital capitalism (Li, 2021).

Nevertheless, the rising free eBooks model has been proven to be more adaptive to the Chinese webnovel and digital reading markets. The 2021 Report on the Development of Online Literature in China highlights that a staggering 46.7 per cent of users have never engaged in content payments. Among different paid content models, only 20 per cent subscribe to unlimited or VIP plans that secure stable revenue sources for paid business (Chinese Academy of Social Sciences, 2022). In such a market, it is challenging for premium paid content providers to maintain stable revenue streams from paying readers.

Other eBook vendors in China also encountered Yuewen's dilemma between free and paid content development. Prior to the rise of ad-supported free eBook apps, the Chinese mobile reading market was dominated by paid platforms: iReader led with a 53 per cent market share in 2018, followed by QQ

Read at 47.5 per cent, and Migu Read at 30 per cent (Graziani, 2018). However, the revenue from paid eBooks has been overshadowed by the rapidly expanding free content market after 2018. For example, the market leader iReader experienced a significant drop of 28.9 per cent in monthly active users between 2019 and 2020, coinciding with rapid growth for free eBook apps (iReader Tech, 2022). In response to this burgeoning trend, iReader launched its own free reading app, Dejian Novel, which earned nearly RMB 200 million (USD 27.5 million) in advertising revenue in 2020, making advertising the primary driver of growth for the company (iReader Tech, 2022). The evident commercial success of the free experiment prompted iReader to transition towards a hybrid approach of 'subscription + free' to manage traffic and amplify its commercial allure deftly.

The rise of ad-supported free models has undeniably transformed the mainstream eBook platforms in China. However, platforms like iReader, which employ a hybrid model, face a challenge in providing distinct offerings for paying and free users. Understandably, many platforms offer cost-effective content with lower licensing fees for free models, compromising on quality. Furthermore, they require more data and privacy compromises from free users to develop targeted advertisements and refine advertising outcomes. In contrast, the paid branch champions itself as a premium content provider and optimises the digital reading experience, making it appealing to paying users. This puts the hybrid system in the problematic situation of both distinguishing paid and free services and balancing reader experience and advertising revenue.

In this landscape, WeChat Read stands out as, perhaps, a unique innovation that addresses the challenge and further advances the integration of free eBooks and the social media ecosystem. Launched in 2015 by Tencent, WeChat Read is primarily a social reading app with a slogan of 'making reading no longer lonely', where users read, share, and discuss eBooks with their contacts on WeChat. Apart from social reading, the big disruption of WeChat Read is its generous user-rewarding system. Specifically, WeChat Read users are able to accumulate rewarding points through engaging in social reading activities, such as sharing reading experiences, inviting friends, or gifting eBooks, and then exchanging these points for unlimited cards to access eBooks for free. While the model might not sound very innovative, the uniqueness of WeChat Read is the ease of gaining free access through participating in reasonably simple social reading tasks. Many bloggers on Zhihu, WeChat, and Weibo shared tips for free digital reading on WeChat Read, explaining how to earn rewarding points and save significant money on books (Hepu, n.d.).

Unlike ad-supported free reading apps that rely on self-published web-novels, the eBooks on WeChat Read are mostly published books with an ISBN and a state-owned publisher imprint, many of which are not freely available on other eBook portals like iReader and Kindle. WeChat Read's eBook catalogue also includes many bestselling or award-winning titles like *Three-Body Problem*, *Kite Runner*, and *To Live*. The eBooks are specifically chosen to cater to WeChat's context of acquaintance social networking, as they are not only meant to be read privately but also shared with real-world contacts such as friends, family, and colleagues, showcasing one's taste in reading.

In 2018, WeChat Read introduced unlimited reading cards for users to exchange their points for, allowing them to access free eBooks across the site. The generous rewards and high-quality eBooks propelled WeChat Read's rapid growth, from 115 million users in 2019 to 210 million in 2020, with an average 50 per cent, thirty-day retention rate, which means half of its users remained actively engaged one month after their initial interaction (Yang et al., 2019). The rapid growth of WeChat Read based on free content undeniably came with a high economic cost, raising the criticism of 'burning money' and concerns about long-term sustainability. This turned out to be particularly insightful when WeChat Read significantly changed the unlimited reading cards and imposed more restrictions on reader-rewarding programmes in 2022, revoking unlimited access to bestselling eBooks and requiring the purchase of premium content or VIP membership. Some thus interpret the free eBook offering on WeChat Read as a bait-and-switch tactic, luring users with free content and subsequently pushing paid versions (Zhang, 2022).

Nevertheless, WeChat Read presents a different business strategy for free eBooks in a broad platform ecosystem, moving beyond the traditional tension between user-paying and advertiser-paying models. It is safe to argue that WeChat Read is not targeting users who cannot afford books but are willing to trade their time and data for free content, like other free reading apps.

According to the statistics released by the company, 84 per cent of WeChat Read users live in first-tier cities, and 79 per cent have a bachelor's degree or higher (Jiang, 2019), which constitutes one of the most valued demographics for advertising, e-commerce, and broad internet business. Furthermore, active users spend an average of eighty-five minutes daily on WeChat Read (Chen, 2020), demonstrating the economic value of digital reading as a time-intensive activity for social media platforms.

The capability of WeChat Read to attract and retain the high-end reading population in the WeChat ecosystem brings new economic values and commercial opportunities. WeChat Read is able to collect data across digital reading and social networking based on users' real-world identities and contacts, allowing the platform to not only offer more targeted and customised content services but also deeply understand users' cultural tastes, intellectual interests, social values, and even political preferences, which would be useful for informing Tencent's content production and broad commercial exploitation (He, 2020). As Tencent is one of the largest producers of digital entertainment content in China, WeChat Read serves as a super access point for transmedia content and a channel for distribution and monetisation. In doing so, WeChat Read keeps adding more related elements in the eBook description, in particular, the various adaptations of popular titles, ranging from audiobooks to comics, games, animations, and web dramas, with hyperlinks directing readers to relevant products or platforms. I will discuss these dynamics in Chapter 4 in relation to the ecosystem strategies of Chinese super apps like WeChat and Douyin. At this stage, however, it is worth highlighting that the innovation of WeChat Read lies in redefining the value proposition of digital reading beyond the eBook business and seeking alternative pathways for sustainable free content models in a broader platform ecosystem.

While iReader and WeChat Read appear to follow different evolutionary trajectories in free eBook developments, both highlight a trend of hybridisation and diversification of digital content revenues. According to QuestMobile (2022), the duration of free digital reading in the mobile internet industry is still increasing rapidly, with a growth rate of over 40 per cent in China in 2022. In other words, the free reading market is far from being saturated. This trend is also evident in the developments of other Chinese eBook vendors.

For instance, NetEase Read tried to embed free digital reading into existing models by allowing users to access any eBook free of charge for the first hour of each day. On the other hand, the Chinese online advertising market has always been competitive. As more platforms join the free eBook market, advertising resources will inevitably become scarce, making it challenging for eBook vendors and digital publishers who remain less experienced and capable in this field than online streaming, gaming, and music platforms. It is one of the reasons that iReader Tech forecasted a drop in net profits by roughly 60 per cent for 2022 (iReader Tech, 2023). Looking ahead, even though the hybrid model may become more prevalent in China's eBook industry, innovative approaches are still needed to improve advertising effectiveness, optimise user experiences, and explore diverse revenue sources in order to ensure long-term sustainability.

2.4 Platform Power and Knowledge Equity

The disruptive innovation driving the evolution of free eBook models in China could be characterised by various practices and shifting dynamics, from controversial experiments by online bookstores to advertisement-supported free reading on mainstream platforms to convergence between digital reading and the social media ecosystem. However, they all demonstrate a paradigm shift in publishing value propositions and book cultures in the context of content overload, attention economy, and access economy (Weel, 2014; Skains, 2019). As such, the eBook business moves away from its traditional role as a distribution and retailing channel based on the scarcity of content. Instead, it is valued for attracting and retaining mass readers in digital reading, moderating digital content for personalised and connected user experience, and exploiting the resources generated through readership and eBook consumption in a broader platform economy. eBook vendors thus operate more like other digital platforms in fields like online news, short video, online music, and games. In other words, the digital publishing business is expected to create new tangible economic value in an expansive digital ecosystem by facilitating creative proliferation and monetising both creative contributions and participatory consumptions through innovative yet complicated business practices.

This shift reflects the notion of convergence and underscores the transformative power of free eBook disruptions, as well as a dynamic confluence of disruptive innovations, business adaptions, and evolving book cultures. In fact, free eBooks innovation is only the surface of China's profound digital publishing evolution, as its developments are built upon and driven by broader transformations, either webnovels' integration with Tencent's pan-entertainment ecosystem or WeChat Read's ambition of reshaping digital reading in the social media ecosystem, which I will further unpack in the following chapters.

Despite the transformative potential, ensuring the benefits of publishers, authors, and readers is important but has yet to be well addressed. The response from the traditional sector is beyond simply resistance, though adaptation and co-evolution may prove challenging. In the free eBook field, the narrative employed by digital innovators to persuade publishers to come on board is twofold. First, offering free eBooks can effectively cultivate digital reading habits with copyrighted content and increase the sale of print books. Second, China's online advertising market provides tremendous opportunitiy in digital publishing where the free eBook platforms could even utilise less-bestselling books to generate significant economic benefits. The Chinese publishers may not buy these arguments. However, the more direct or practical reason they are open to free experiments lies in the comparatively small proportion of eBook sales (about 5 per cent) in total revenues (Open Book, 2023). Even so, Chinese publishers are trying to retain the final say regarding access to their titles in the platform-mediated system for free eBooks. This means withdrawing from free experiments and fighting for a reasonable share of commercial and economic benefits in the emerging free economy. For example, new Classics, a leading trade book publisher, decided to withdraw all eBook titles from the WeChat Read platform in 2020 due to concerns about its free model (Liu, 2020). While there is no publicly available data on advertising revenue distribution among platforms and publishers, the signs can be read from industry discourses and corporate releases. For example, iReader's annual report indicates that the cost of obtaining eBook content has increased significantly (iReader Tech, 2023), reflecting publishers' growing awareness of their economic interests and bargaining power in the advertising-supported free eBook business. Additionally, publishers and authors should demand more transparency on how their free eBooks are moderated and monetised, especially in light of the algorithmic influence in content discovery and advertising performance.

Besides economic factors, China's free eBook development plays a significant social role by expanding public access to knowledge and digital readership, particularly among less educated and low-income demographics. Undeniably, the quality of free eBooks and the value of digital reading have become a target of criticism, particularly given that self-published entertaining webnovels have become the major content source. In the early 2010s, the top bestsellers on China Mobile Reading Base were light novels and cheap stories, many of which contained explicit pornographic content. There was also a mocking industry saying then that listed securities, nannies, and cleaners as the 'three representatives' of digital readers. However, the social value of free eBooks exists in attracting people like manual workers and rural migrants who did not read in the print age into the eBook world. By creating a burgeoning new reading market, free eBooks serve as a catalyst socially, democratising reading and literature in China.

The scale and innovation of China's free eBook evolution may present a unique case, largely attributing to special contextual elements like weak copyright enforcement, less modernised print publishing, and public attitudes towards paid content. However, the digital disruption of free eBooks is also part of the global evolution of digital content industries. For example, Netflix and Disney Plus added a cheaper ad-supported plan in 2022 after the growing cancellation rate of their previous subscription plans (Spangler, 2022). Spotify recently allowed paid users to try out as many audiobooks as they want for fifty hours each month (Khalid, 2023), which embedded a complimentary component in a similar way to NetEase Read. In an uncertain post-pandemic economy characterised by rising living costs and possible economic recessions, digital content industries, including eBooks, may have to embrace free content alternatives to secure business sustainability. This also makes free content models, as well as the business logic focusing on accessibility and affordability, more valuable socially to ensure knowledge equity. China's free eBook evolution may thus offer some valuable lessons not only for business innovations but also for open and inclusive publishing for disadvantaged populations, making books not a luxury for them.

3 Labour and Power in Platformed Webnovels

3.1 Beyond Digital Self-Publishing

A 2016 article published in the *New York Times*, during the peak of China's webnovel boom, used the phrase 'people's literature' to celebrate this emerging yet disruptive form of literary creation, specifically lauding its greater freedom for expression, with 'fewer restrictions', 'less pressure', and 'very few commercial elements' in the writing process (Qin, 2016). Webnovel, also known as online literature, is a type of born-digital, self-published literary work, typically serialised genre fiction, with featuring components of social storytelling and participatory fandom, which has evolved into a digital publishing industry with an economic scale of nearly USD 4 billion in China today (Ren, 2023). It is not surprising that webnovel received positive appraisals for creative liberalisation amid the digital optimism of the Web 2.0 era, which accentuated the emancipatory potential and empowerment of individual creators and networked readers. However, the article seems to neglect that the phrase 'people's literature' carries connotations rooted in the context of the Communist literary system as a mechanism for advancing revolutionary objectives and political ideologies, often at the expense of individual liberty. Thus, the discourse presents an interesting yet compelling juxtaposition between the optimistic industry narrative and the economic, social, and political contexts of digital publishing in China, which is constrained in many aspects.

A few years later, Chinese literary critic Bai Ye, while commenting on the annual webnovel rankings in 2020, invoked the term 'people's literature' drawing on the tradition of Socialist realism (Clark, 1984), arguing that the core of webnovels is people's literature and as such online writers should 'engage with the ordinary people for inspiration, utilise people's collective experiences as a foundational reference, and source the materials from the broad spectrum of people's real-life' (Liu & Yan, 2020). Bai's reorientation echoes the extant government policy that advocates a transition in the thematic focus of webnovels from predominantly entertainment-centric genres driven by commercial platforms, such as fantasy, alternative history, science fiction, and supernatural stories, towards a 'main melody' approach that foregrounds realistic and ideologically resonant themes (China Literature, 2022).

The realm of webnovels is perhaps one of the most globally publicised yet frequently misinterpreted facets of China's digital publishing landscape, partially due to the challenge of defining it as both the echo of Western digital self-publishing and China's monumental digital innovations with its own characteristics. Chinese webnovel, as digital literary innovation, is not unique. There are various parallel developments elsewhere, ranging from social storytelling sites like Wattpad in Canada to community-oriented self-publishing sites like Shōsetsuka ni Narōmobile in Japan. However, the uniqueness of China's webnovel evolution lies in its long transformative trajectory spanning over twenty years, from a grassroots disruption to a vast-scale, highly industrialised, platform-based, and politically censored digital publishing ecosystem. There is thus a need to move beyond simplification, either industry narrative or government propaganda, to reflect the real dynamism and complexity of the field, in particular, the interplay between the liberalising possibilities afforded by disruptive publishing models and the constraints arising from commercial and political contexts in China, ranging from the dominance of platforms as infrastructural intermediaries to governmental control of literary creation. Central to the interplay are fundamental issues of labour and power, which underlie the contesting interpretations of the phrase 'people's literature' and exhibit the evolving power dynamics between creative publics, platforms, and government in digital authoring and publishing. Webnovel thus offers a uniquely valuable case to understand and contextualise the disruptive innovations and their impact on China's eBook evolution, as well as their global implications beyond Chinese characteristics.

This chapter aims to offer a refreshed and evolving perspective on the labour and power of Chinese platformed webnovels, drawing on its over twenty years' evolution. It starts with a chronological mapping of webnovel developments from the 1990s to the present, traversing from grassroots disruptions to platformisation to the digital entertainment ecosystem. This serves to contextualise the subsequent focus of networked writing publics, where the chapter explores the multifaceted roles of webnovel authors, ranging from participatory fan-creators to content entrepreneurs and precarious labourers in the eBook economy. The third part further explores the shifting power dynamics among stakeholders, addressing a central question of who benefits and dominates during these disruptive transformations. Finally, the chapter extends its analysis beyond the Chinese context and conceptualises self-publishing as a vital source of cheap creative labour in a disruptive digital economy, providing disruptors with content resources to challenge established models, which sheds new light on our understanding of the next wave of disruption driven by generative AI.

3.2 Three Evolutionary Stages of Webnovels

3.2.1 The Age of Grassroots Disruption

The emergence of webnovels is driven by both the universal dynamic of digital self-publishing and China's own cultural, economic, and social transitions. In the print age, self-publishing was synonymous with vanity press, where authors had to make significant upfront investments in producing physical books due to a perceived lack of quality or marketability. However, digital self-publishing, harnessing social networks, participatory culture, and fan economy, is building an alternative or parallel universe, without publishers' gatekeeping and corporate control, for content creation, circulation, and consumption (Jenkins et al., 2013; Thompson, 2021). The webnovel developments in the early years in China largely reflected such optimism as new models were challenging both established literary institutions and government censorship.

Chinese webnovels started to boom in the 1990s when a growing number of amateur writers and fans began to share their stories online, like elsewhere in the world. The uniqueness in China, though, is that its print literary publishing industry was tightly controlled by the government and constrained to elitist literary forms. Thus, it failed to meet the growing market demands for entertaining genre fiction in China (Ren & Montgomery, 2012; Shao, 2023). This created opportunities for online writers, who leveraged the comparatively uncensored space to produce and disseminate genre stories alongside various literary forms. The circumvention of gatekeeping measures imposed by traditional publishers, government censors, and literary authorities has led to an unprecedented diversity of literary expression in Chinese online literature in its early grassroots age (Hockx, 2015), in which webnovels played a significant part.

Online writing then also exhibited an extraordinary level of collaboration, exemplified by the pioneering *Nine Continents* series – a set of fantasy novels based on a shared mythological universe. It was a milestone in webnovel evolution that showcased the immense potential of massive collaborative online writing. In 2001, author Bubble invited contributors to the Qingyun Forum to co-create a Western-style fantasy world, which attracted hundreds of active Chinese-speaking contributors worldwide. Interestingly, the collective endeavour soon shifted into constructing a uniquely Chinese fantasy universe embedded with Eastern mythology and history. As such, the utopian experiment led to the creation of China's first, born-digital, extensive, alternate universe for storytelling, organised into nine continents inhabited by six races – an imaginary also reflecting and symbolising real-world societal tensions. Although the Nine Continents Creation Alliance ultimately dissolved due to internal discord, its lasting impact on the fantasy webnovel genre is undeniable. The alliance yielded an array of exceptional webnovels based on the collectively created universe. Several of these, including *Jiu Zhou: The Skyscraper of Cloud Raising* (by Jinhezai) and *Jiu Zhou: The Mystic Record* (by Jiangnan), have endured as genre-defining works in the Chinese fantasy webnovels.

The age of grassroots disruption witnessed the proliferation of hundreds of bulletin board systems (BBS), forums, and websites dedicated to online writing, most of which faded into history in later years. Rongshuxia, for example, launched in 1997, established itself as a non-commercial, community-oriented sanctuary where amateur writers could explore a spectrum of online literature forms, including webnovels. Tianya Forum, a long-standing pillar in China's digital public sphere, was renowned for its wide-ranging public dialogues, including dedicated zones to online literature and supernatural stories, where several top-ranked webnovels like *Ghost Blow Lamp* were initially published. As webnovels and online publishing were still in their infancy, these sites unsurprisingly operated on an ad–revenue model without staking a commercial claim in the content. Based on free online content, numerous writers like Li Xunhuan, Tianxia Bachang, and

Dangnian Mingyue accumulated significant popularity, making them best-selling authors in the print book publishing industry. As such, the financial gains from popular webnovels went to the traditional publishing sector with mature business systems, while online sites struggled financially long term by not capitalising on the value of the webnovel content they mediated.

Unlike Rongshuxia and Tianya, another pivotal player in webnovel history, Qidian sought to generate revenue directly through online reading, eventually revolutionising the Chinese webnovel industry. Launched by a group of fantasy lovers in 2002, mostly university students, Qidian invented a unique business model combining freemium and micropayment, which allowed readers to access the initial chapters for free but charged them for reading premium content on a chapter-by-chapter basis. Despite scepticism initially, the model enabled online writers to earn real money from webnovel writing for the first time in history – a previously unimaginable scenario. Moreover, compared with voluntary crowdsourcing by readers of free content, the dollar votes turned out to be a more reliable and effective mechanism to harness readers' collective intelligence to filter high-quality webnovels. Subscription income and readers' selection have later become two pillars of webnovel business for both Qidian and the industry at large, ensuring the best works and authors are recognised and rewarded directly by their fans (Ren, 2016).

It is worth mentioning that no matter what business logic and models these sites employed, renowned writers with dedicated fans constituted the most valuable economic resource in the author-centred webnovel industry in the era of grassroots disruption. Most websites, including Qidian, ardently sought to attract and retain these popular writers, for which they willingly compromised their immediate economic interests (Shao, 2023). This sharply contrasts with the current platform-dominated environment, where authors are compelled to relinquish extensive rights to the platform that mediates content and controls reader access (Global Times, 2020), which will be discussed in Chapter 3.3.

3.2.2 Commercialisation in the Platform Age

The process of platformisation in China's webnovel industry has been led by two major corporations: Shengda Literature and Yuewen Group. By transforming webnovels from a community-based, participatory literary sphere into a realm of the platformed and industrialised publishing business, these companies also turned into new types of publishers. In the West, self-publishing platforms like Draft2Digital, PublishDrive, and StreetLib mainly operate as aggregators and service providers supporting self-published authors for a fee. Even in models like KDP, the platform's role is primarily an intermediary. However, Chinese companies such as Shengda and Yuewen are much more involved in the digital publishing business as both infrastructural intermediaries and digital publishers. They hold copyrights for webnovels published on their platforms, mentor contracted authors, conduct editorial control, and generate revenue from eBook sales, online advertising, transmedia adaptations, and IP franchising. Such an industrial structure resulted from a complex evolutionary process of industrialisation and platformisation of webnovels in China.

In 2005, Shanda Corporation acquired Qidian, the leading webnovel site, and subsequently acquired other major competitors, including Hongxiu Tianxiang, Jinjiang, Romance Novel Bar, and Rongshuxia over the following years. These acquisitions marked the end of the grassroots era and the start of industrialisation in this emerging field, characterised by monopolistic control of Shengda over the once-open landscape. Driven by platform publishers, webnovels were deeply industrialised in two ways: the establishment of a comprehensive genre system for content production and the normalisation of Qidian's business model based on freemium and micropayment.

The consolidation of webnovel sites under Shengda Corporation enables the standardisation of webnovel storytelling, leading to an elaborate system of genres and sub-genres, facilitating assembly line replication of popular storylines and narrative techniques. Undeniably, the webnovels' genre system transcends the traditional categories such as fantasy, romance, adventure, and wuxia by generating and refining a range of novel genres and sub-genres like Tomb Robbery, Time-Travel Romance, Alternative History, Boy Love Stories, Romance with CEOs, and Eastern Fantasy. Additionally, leading platforms often tailor their storytelling to target either male or female audiences specifically; for instance, Qidian is popular among male readers, while Jinjiang is primarily for female readers. Under such a system, each webnovel is categorised under specific genre tags and adheres to established genre formulas in storytelling, worldbuilding, and character development. With the help of big data technologies and advanced algorithms, webnovel platforms become capable of identifying and defining genres and providing personalised recommendations to users effectively (Xu, 2021). While this helps retain a loyal readership, the automated genre system allows algorithms to significantly influence the discoverability, visibility, and popularity of webnovels.

Concurrently, Qidian has set an industrial business standard with its freemium, chapter-based micropayment model. The platforms offer initial chapters for free to attract readers while generating revenue from payments for subsequent chapters. Under such a business system, individual writers have to release chapters every day and produce lengthy, serialised novels with intricate world-building, numerous characters, and protracted story-lines to keep readers engaged. As a result, webnovels tend to be volumi-nous, ranging between two and four million words, and take years to complete.

The widespread adoption of the genre system and chapter-based reader-paying model has led to the rapid growth of the webnovel industry, recording its highest annual revenue increase of 51.7 per cent in 2015 (Statista, 2023). However, profitability remained elusive for most compa-nies. According to the IPO file of Shengda released in 2012, the company had net losses in 2009–2011, 'primarily due to copyright licensing cost, head-count related expenses and sales and marketing expenses' required to operate the business in the early stages (Cloudary Corporation, 2012). Like other eBook industries, increasing the number of paying users has been a challenge. While webnovel companies attributed it largely to piracy, claiming the pirated sites generated ten times the revenue of legitimate operations, questions about the sustainability of a business model relying on reader payments have been raised (Ren & Montgomery, 2012).

The turning point of business evolution was the so-called Super IP craze that took off around 2014, quickly becoming a buzzword within China's digital publishing and creative industries. Super IP refers to intellectual properties from highly popular creative works with a substantial audience or fanbase (Ren, 2016). In both the burgeoning mobile phone gaming industry and the television sector, there has been a surge in the adaptation of popular webnovels into games and TV dramas. This trend gained momentum following the commercial successes of hit TV shows based on webnovels around 2014–2015, such as *Scarlet Heart* and *Empresses in the Palace*, making webnovel industry attractive to film/TV producers, investors, and cultural enterprises who saw substantial commercial potential in capitalising on the intellectual property rights. The heightened interest resulted in elevated levels of investment in the adaptations of webnovels. Consequently, high-profile works with the status of 'Super IP' were adapted into diverse media forms, ranging from films to TV dramas, comics, animations, games, and audiobooks. This wide-ranging exploitation of webnovel IPs undoubtedly bears historical semblances to their Western counterparts in genre fiction and comic books, where literary publishing is perceived as the audiences' initial entry point into a content franchise (Murray, 2012). Additionally, the 'Super IP' developments of webnovels in China also contributed to refashioning the television industry and boosting emerging video streaming platforms (Bai, 2019).

To the webnovel industry that faced financial challenges with reader-paying models then, adaptation and franchising offered an important alternative revenue source. The substantial income generated from IP operations, as well as the fervour for IP investments, even shifted the business models and creative practices as authors started to change story genres and writing styles to be more suitable for transmedia adaptation, expecting to generate more revenues from selling adaptation rights (Ren, 2016). However, the Super IP fervour also caused issues such as inflated IP prices, lack of rational decision-making in acquisitions, and hoarding of IPs, hindering the healthy development of the industry (Tang, 2019). Furthermore, back in the mid-2010s, Shengda was primarily a gaming company and had yet to establish a comprehensive entertainment ecosystem to maximise the opportunities for franchising and adaptations.

The seminal industrial shift occurred in 2015 when Shengda Literature was acquired for RMB 5 billion (USD 684 million) by Yuewen Group, then a newly established subsidiary of the Chinese internet giant Tencent. The rationale behind it was an evolutionary leap in the underlying business model and strategic vision for the IP-driven webnovel economy. Whereas webnovels were previously regarded as an extension of the traditional literary book business, Tencent's entry signalled an emerging paradigm of webnovel as a crucial component of an integrated digital entertainment ecosystem.

3.2.3 The Age of Digital Entertainment Ecosystem

The reason behind Tencent's acquisition of webnovel enterprises is closely linked to its pan-entertainment strategy, which, initiated in 2015, has a broad vision beyond the confines of the single content industry. Pan-entertainment encompasses a wide range of digital content and entertainment sectors, such as social media, web/TV dramas, games, music, and animation, facilitating the exchange and convergence of traffic, content, and financial resources across platforms (Wang, 2021). China's permissive regulatory landscape in relation to cross-media ownership has enabled Tencent to acquire and own a diverse portfolio of media enterprises across sectors, thereby erecting an entertainment empire that Disney and Hollywood would envy (Li, 2017). Such a conducive environment amplifies the potential for cultivating an IP-centric, ecosystem-driven, and cross-subsidised network for upgraded webnovel business.

The economic value of webnovels is also being recognised as a primary source of original content or stories driving the ecosystem built upon Tencent's prominent role in both the Chinese video streaming market (via Tencent Video) and the global gaming industry (via Tencent Game) (Liu, 2021). While webnovels may not be positioned strategically at the centre of the Tencent ecosystem, the IP franchising and adaptations are no longer confined to standalone TV dramas or films but involve the creation of a transmedia universe that provides multi-layered storytelling experiences, engaging audiences through a variety of media formats (Frater, 2018). Such a transformative approach would lead to restructuring and extension of the webnovel value chain, thereby creating multiple channels for distribution, monetisation, and franchising.

In line with this strategic vision, webnovel platforms owned by Yuewen, having gained privileged access to Tencent's super apps of QQ and WeChat, leverage the social networking infrastructure to significantly increase fan engagement, create thriving online communities for webnovels, and offer readers personalised yet connected experiences based on their social data (Chen, 2017). Additionally, Tencent Video, the dominant streaming platform like Netflix in China, has become a major distribution channel for transmedia content adapted from Yuewen's webnovels. In 2017, some of Yuewen's heavyweight intellectual properties (IPs), including *Fighter of the Destiny*, *The King's Avatar*, and *Noble Aspirations*, were adapted into TV/web dramas and animations, generating revenue of RMB 366 million (USD 50 million) in IP operation and franchising (China Literature, 2018). In 2018, Yuewen acquired New Classics Media to produce transmedia content based on its own popular webnovels, aiming to internalise IP content creation and reduce dependence on third-party content production. This move boosted economic performance significantly, as the annual revenue generated from IP operations surged to RMB 4.42 billion (USD 600 million) in the year after the acquisition, invigorated by the commercial success of high-calibre works such as *The Untamed* and *Joy of Life* (China Literature, 2022). The year 2019 also marked a turning point in Yuewen's financial structure as, for the first time, income from intellectual property (IP) operations exceeded digital reading revenue, accounting for 53 per cent of the total revenue (Chen, 2022). As the largest company in the industry, the shift also indicates a transformation of the webnovel economy from an eBook and publishing business predicated on reader-paying models to a transmedia IP industry integral to the digital entertainment ecosystem.

Despite having long dominated the webnovel industry, Yuewen's adaptation business is facing intense competition from other tech giants such as ByteDance, particularly in the emerging short video field. In recent years, mini-dramas have become a growingly lucrative genre on short video platforms like Douyin and Kuaishou (Ji, 2023). As a new type of low-cost production, mini-dramas usually have hundreds of episodes, each lasting less than three minutes. Short video platforms like Douyin tried to establish a strategic alliance between free eBooks and mini-dramas. For instance, Douyin launched an official channel called Tomato Mini Theatre in August 2020 for mini-dramas adapted from the popular webnovels published with its free eBook platform Tomato Novel. Likewise, Kuaishou partnered with Midu Read, another leading free eBook app, aiming to adapt webnovels into mini-dramas to enhance its short video content offering.

Douyin and Kuaishou adopted a different approach from Yuewen in the field of mini-dramas, which tend to adapt webnovels that have moderate popularity or are freely available instead of top-tier flagship works (Yan, 2020). This cost-effective approach creates a new path for monetising such works and offers mid-tier or average authors, who were neglected in the Super IP developments, opportunities to earn through IP operations.

The rise of mini-dramas and free eBooks apps is bringing significant commercial benefits to ByteDance's Douyin ecosystem, positioning it as a strong competitor to Tencent's pan-entertainment developments. To cope with the competitive pressure from competing tech giants, a new strategy called 'Big Yuewen' was proposed by Yuewen's new CEO, Cheng Wu, in 2020:

> [I]nstead of lone ships in a vast ocean, IPs should be seen as a fleet, mutually supporting and empowering each other. By synthesising elements of industrialisation, systematisation, and standardisation, an ecosystem centred on IPs can be formed, which can counteract inherent uncertainties in the industry. (Liu, 2021)

Although Cheng Wu was succeeded by his deputy, Cheng Xiaonan, in 2023, the 'Big Yuewen' strategy remains the cornerstone of the company's business practice, now augmented by an even more ambitious vision of leveraging AI technology to cultivate a sustainable and healthy webnovel community and IP ecosystem (Hu, 2023). While the current power dynamics still favour Yuewen (DoNews, 2020), the competing forces supported by ByteDance are introducing innovative, disruptive strategies, thereby furthering the industry's transition towards a cross-platform, trans-media, and diversely financed entertainment ecosystem, which will profoundly shape the future of webnovels.

3.3 Networked Writing Publics

As of 2022, there were 22.8 million registered online writers on various platforms in China, and writing webnovel became a preferred form of secondary employment among the Chinese online publics, earning supplementary income through literary creation (Chinese Academy of Social Sciences, 2023). The sheer scale of this burgeoning writing publics indicates a disruptive yet democratising process of literary expression, as well as a novel, capitalist approach to mobilising, organising, and commercialising population-wide creativity in a platform economy. As already discussed, the business practices of webnovel industry have undergone sequential phases of disruption, platformisation, and ecosystem-driven integration over the past decades, where webnovels have broadly transformed from a grassroots movement with promises of democratisation and diversification to platformed digital publishing deeply shaped by the hegemony of tech giants in every aspect of creation and communication.

In this Element, I define the webnovel writers as 'networked writing publics', drawing on Kazys' (2012) concept of networked publics and Ryder's (2011) work on writing publics. By this term, I hope to emphasise the population-wide literary creation and the diverse publics involved in the webnovel evolution, which diverges from the conventional understanding of writers that often encapsulates an elitist, privileged perspective on those deemed worthy of literary creation. Such networked writing publics could be further classified into three distinct yet overlapping categories in the webnovel context: participatory fan-creators who write for fun, content entrepreneurs who manage to thrive in the platformed literary market, and precarious labourers motivated primarily by direct income from the platforms.

Most famous webnovel authors started their journey as fans, motivated by passion in a particular genre, with little expectation of monetary rewards. Webnovels, as a social, participatory, and collaborative form of literary production, also foster a communal environment where authors are more willing to contribute their affective labour to the fan community, facilitated by the dynamic interplay between creators and fans on both webnovel platforms and social media (Tang et al., 2022). While hobby-driven writing was prevalent in the early grassroots age when commercialisation was hard to achieve, the recent study interestingly re-emphasises the motivation of personal satisfaction and pleasure among online writers, evidenced by 67.7 per cent of survey respondents liked or strongly liked their job despite the precarious employment (He et al., 2022). This pattern could be further attributed to the demographic of webnovel authors, where the post-95s generation has risen to become the group with the largest proportion and fastest growth (Chinese Academy of Social Sciences, 2022). These people are devoted into online writing as they do not have a life burden; they are mostly unmarried one-child generation and financially supported by their families (He et al., 2022). This may sound like a disheartening fact in today's commercialised webnovel sector, incongruent with the idyllic industry narrative of online writing as both fun and reputation/wealth building, which aims to attract aspiring authors to the field (Ren, 2020).

Webnovel authorship has been profoundly influenced by industrialisation in China, despite the dynamic of population-wide public writing and the initial motivation of leisure and fandom. The creators are encouraged, or arguably required, to adopt an entrepreneurial mindset towards creative practices, echoing the broader neoliberal ideology of normalising individual entrepreneurialism (Banet-Weiser, 2011). As such, writing webnovels, once seen as a largely solitary and self-driven pursuit, now takes on the characteristics of running a start-up business. Webnovel business directly offers two ways of remuneration for writers through platform intermediation: profit sharing with platforms based on the number of paid subscriptions and the direct gift or money given by loyal fans (He et al., 2022). The commercial opportunities have also been advanced by transmedia convergence, super IP operations, and digital entertainment ecosystems, with diverse pathways for writing publics to gain economic benefits. The rise of free eBooks and mini-dramas especially widens the access for average webnovel authors to expand their revenue streams through online advertising, adaptations, and IP franchising. In such a business environment, producing appealing and engaging content remains essential, but successful online writers are expected to find ways to establish and maintain a popular presence, engage with and retain readers in their stories, and accumulate, manage, and monetise their popularity as an entrepreneur (Hu, 2020). There are various examples where grassroots creators changed their lives through commercialised webnovel writing and entrepreneurial endeavours. To them, webnovel writing can serve as merely a starting point of the entrepreneurial journey, whereby they start to accumulate popularity and leveraged and monetised cultural capital in a broader platform-based creative economy.

While this vision is appealing, the majority of webnovel authors unavoidably work as cheap labourers in the process of commercialising individual creativity. Webnovel writing certainly has another face as a stressful, precarious, and low-paying job, inherently stemming from consumer labour entrepreneurship (Zhang & Fung, 2014). A 2016 survey revealed that a substantial 80 per cent of online writers in China could not sustain themselves solely through their literary output; a mere 20 per cent exceeded a monthly income of RMB 10,000 (USD 1,367), commonly viewed as the threshold for high earnings in an urban context then (NetEase Cloud Reading, 2016). The report by iResearch (2018) further corroborates the income dissatisfaction, revealing that among top-tier (5-star) authors, only 23.7 per cent were very satisfied and 43.5 per cent satisfied, while among those rated between two and four stars, the figures dropped to a mere 5.2 per cent very satisfied and 26.2 per cent satisfied. Apart from dissatisfactory income, participants in a high-profile industry forum raised various concerns relating to the working conditions and well-being of webnovel authors in the platformed, stressful online writing environment, including physical and mental health issues, the absence of job stability, limited access to social welfare systems, and extended working hours (Xu, 2021), which reflect profound concerns around webnovel writing as digital creative labour. All these issues indicate a lure of exploitation, particularly given that Chinese webnovel authors averagely have five years of experience in the industry (Chinese Academy of Social Sciences, 2023).

The power imbalance between writing publics and platforms could be further demonstrated by the exploitative contractual terms, known as 'Literary Transfer Agreements', used as a standard legal document by major webnovel sites since 2009. These terms deprived authors of their adaptation rights, gave the platform the authority to license their copyrights and distribute content without consent or revenue sharing, and even gave the platform unilateral control over the authors' social media accounts (Global Times, 2020; Zhang, 2020). Such an agreement is undeniably detrimental to authors, especially when their works achieve significant popularity. For example, Zhang Muye, a popular webnovelist known as Tianxia Bachang, had to take legal action to regain the right to use characters from his highly ranked webnovel, *Ghost Blows Light*, in a new work. This case highlights the controversial nature of such contractual terms and the restrictions they imposed on authors' legal rights and creative liberties (Liang, 2019). Adding to the controversy, these contracts, usually signed after the online publication of an initial 10,000 words, require the author to adhere to a predetermined writing plan based on genre norms and stereotypical plotlines; otherwise, the platform can suspend or terminate the agreement (Global Times, 2020).

Confronting such a system, webnovel authors employed diverse strategies to respond, ranging from adaption to negotiation to escape, leading to variations in their professional identity and creative practices (Hu, 2020). However, a watershed moment occurred on 5 May 2020, termed 'No Updating Day', when thousands of authors affiliated with Yuewen Group ceased updating their works in protest against inequitable contractual terms, which was further amplified by hundreds of thousands of Weibo posts with the hashtag from fans and readers, attracting over 100 million views (Chen, 2020). These protests eventually led to some revisions of standard author contracts by Yuewen Group, including some controversial terms on authors' rights. Although progress has been made towards fairer contracts, comprehensive protection of authors' revenues and rights in China's evolving webnovel economy still requires significant further improvement.

This Element conceptualises webnovel authors as 'networked writing publics', but it does not echo the narrative viewing webnovel writing as simply side hustle or a hobby (Chinese Academy of Social Sciences, 2023), as it would romanticise webnovel authorship and downplay the economic exploitation by blurring the boundary between leisure and work, labour and consumption, community and commerce (Scholz, 2012; Zhang & Fung, 2014). Rather, by defining webnovel writers as the networked writing publics, this work aims to recognise the scale of population-wide creativity and the multifaceted roles of individual creators as fans, entrepreneurs, and labourers. More importantly, by highlighting the networked and communal nature of online writing, it demands a delicate balance between the contradictory realities of creativity and commerce and a stronger voice for authors in the governance of the digital self-publishing economy.

3.4 The Control of Government and Platform

The rapid growth of webnovels, coupled with their expanding cultural impact, has inevitably led to increased content censorship and governmental control in China, evolving to levels of control comparable to those in the traditional publishing sector, including a range of regulatory measures from compulsory real-name verification of authors to editorial and algorithmic gatekeeping, in addition to regular 'cleaning the web' campaigns aimed at sanitising online content. There is also a noticeable transformation of regulatory mechanisms from a passive approach to censoring 'unhealthy' and sensitive material to an active strategy aimed at directing the digital publishing agenda. Concurrently, the Chinese censors are also mobilising online communities and peer-based surveillance in participatory censorship (Luo & Li, 2022).

Much like banning books in the print era, governmental censors and platform editors regularly delete webnovels that violate censorship rules regarding pornography, politics, and violence. Furthermore, webnovels with topics and portrayals considered politically or socially sensitive, based on standards that are often arbitrary and fluctuating, could also be banned for no explicit reasons (Ren, 2020). Not only individual webnovels but also the entire genre or sub-genre could be banned. For instance, the genre of Chinese officialdom was totally removed from webnovel platforms in 2018 due to concerns about exposing government corruption and sensitive political issues (Jiang, 2018). The heavy government intervention and destructive censorship measures are viewed as a big threat to the industry's sustainability. In 2019, the news of tightened censorship of webnovels immediately led to a significant decline in the stock price of Yuewen (Meng, 2019). To avoid a possible government-mandated shutdown, platforms have implemented proactive gatekeeping measures, in particular, using automation technologies to detect and filter content based on a large number of sensitive words, rendering many normal sentences unpublishable. In some extremely stringent circumstances, webnovel writers have reported that out of their one-hour writing time, only twenty minutes were spent on actual creation, while the remaining forty minutes were on figuring out how to pass online censorship (He, 2020).

The disruptive nature of webnovels engenders a paradoxical dilemma for writing publics: 'The more popular you become, the harder the censors are to please' (O'Neill, 2015). There is a growing trend of depoliticising digital entertainment content in China, driven by a mix of self-censorship and market forces. Webnovel stories, however, despite appearing to be apolitical, inevitably address various social issues and engage with topical matters in China's digital public sphere with a political attitude (Han & Huang, 2019). The market-driven nature and attached political components make webnovels a frequent target of internet censorship and extensive deletion. In the Xi Jinping era, punishment is even imposed on individual authors. Lady Tianyi, for example, a female webnovel author, gets more than ten years in prison for producing and selling the so-called gay pornography, a punishment even more severe than sexual assault cases in China (Hernández & Zhang, 2018).

In addition to massive deletion and individual punishment, the Chinese government is gradually developing a strategy of integrating entertainment with propaganda in digital arts and literature, demonstrated by a series of encouragement policies and material rewards for the creation of 'main melody' or 'positive energy' content. He Hong (2022), a senior official responsible for overseeing online literature within the Chinese Writers Association, articulates the official preferences and objections to authors as follows:

> Harmful cultural elements such as historical nihilism, Danmei (boys' love stories), ostentatious displays of wealth, and tendencies like 'lying flat' (Tang Ping) have not been completely eradicated and, in some cases, even influence reading habits. This necessitates that online writers further elevate their awareness, maintain vigilance, resolutely discard distorted aesthetic inclinations, and proactively shape characters that epitomise the zeitgeist – dignified, robust, progressive, and unpretentious.

Yuewen, as the industry leader, has signalled its intent to align closely with governmental policies and direct guidance, focusing on fostering so-called realistic stories. As detailed in its 2021 Annual Report, the company announced the establishment of the inaugural CCP Party building base for online writers in May 2021. Integral to this inauguration was a delegation of webnovel authors visiting Yan'an, the symbolic birthplace of modern Chinese communism. The initiative served to 'imbue the creative process with the Spirit of Yan'an, whilst simultaneously advocating for high-quality cultural development' in the production of main-melody webnovels (China Literature, 2022:108).

While divergences persist between government and platforms across the world, the Chinese platform economy shows a distinct fusion of state power and capital, making tech giants like Tencent and ByteDance pivotal architects of China's digital economy and society. This Element incorporates a consistent theme to elaborate on the power and influence of platform companies and tech giants in China's digital publishing evolution. In the context of webnovels, the fusion of government and platform powers is twofold. On the one hand, there was unprecedented tolerance of some previously banned genres like supernatural stories, gang crime, and soft porn, which substantially contributed to the industry's rapid expansion in the early years (Ren, 2020). On the other hand, censorship and control remain prevalent as governmental entities and platforms form a symbiotic partnership, with platforms responsible for practical censorship tasks on a daily basis. The Chinese tech crackdown around 2021 (Wu, 2022) significantly enhanced governmental power, resulting in webnovel platforms' increasing acquiescence to and compliance with governmental directives in content moderation, as mentioned in Chapter 1.

In short, the evolution of Chinese webnovels exhibits a complex and evolving interplay between platforms, government, and creative publics. Instead of simply disrupting legacy publishing through democratising writing and empowering creators, China's webnovel evolution presents a new approach to control and a new model of exploitation, incorporating market capitalism and government censorship. Creators' voice remains weak, demonstrated by their depowered position and unfavourable working conditions, as well as the shrinking space for creative practices and diverse expression allowed by the government and platform capital (Yu, 2017). As such, the promise of democratisation through digital self-publishing is inherently fragile, as it depends on a delicate balance of power and ongoing negotiation between writers, readers, platforms, and government, and a middle ground between liberal and controlled approaches in China.

3.5 Cheap Labour and eBook Disruption

China's webnovel evolution occurs in a broader digital creative economy, where disruptive transformation is engendered and deeply shaped by its dependence on cheap labour and vast consumption, the Party-State's disciplinary power and the digital capital's 'biopolitical mode of governing' (Ong, 2006:6; Zhang & Fung, 2014). While the Chinese complexity can contextualise digital self-publishing in various ways, its core economic value lies in the provision of cheap creative labour and affordable original content to meet the vast demands of an emerging reading market. Digital self-publishing is, by nature, an industry of cognitive surplus and hope labour (Shirky, 2010). Both existed in print publishing, normally aligned with the vast volume of 'unpublishable' content rejected by traditional publishers. However, webnovel platforms serve as an intermediary connecting creative hope labour with emerging reading publics. Like free eBook models that thrived by attracting those who did not read in print, webnovel platforms started by mobilising those who were not able to publish in print. It is worth noting that the free eBook initiatives like China Mobile Reading Base, Midu Read, and Tomato Novels all initially relied on webnovels as major content sources to build and grow their business, as traditional publishers resisted licensing published books to these platforms then. As such, webnovels created by cheap creative labour became a vital content source fuelling disruptive innovations in China's eBook evolution.

In the age of the digital entertainment ecosystem, webnovels also serve as a testing ground for original story ideas that could be subsequently adapted and exploited across the entire media spectrum. The sheer diversity and volume of webnovels allowed rapid iteration and consumer validation of countless concepts, allowing pan-entertainment corporations like Tencent to gauge market viability without betting big budgets on unproven ideas or unknown IPs. Instead, they harness cheap creative labour in the webnovel sector to handle the classic challenge in media economics: the uncertainty of entertainment markets (Araman & Popescu, 2010). A reservoir of audience-validated stories is thus built for adaption across media forms. However, in the market-testing process, the risks fall almost entirely on individual authors. If their works are not popular, they earn little to no economic rewards despite the time and creativity invested in their creations.

This chapter conceptualises webnovel disruption from the perspective of producing, governing, and empowering creative labour, and revisits the discourses around digital self-publishing as either a 'giant disruption' (Filloux, 2012) or a romanticised notion of 'people's literature' (Qin, 2016). Unlike a hybrid system of legacy publishers and self-publishing companies in the Western market, the webnovel platforms owned by Yuewen and other platform companies have displaced traditional publishers in many important literary publishing fields. Most literary authors have to gain popularity online before their works can be recognised by print publishers, and their revenue mainly comes from online publishing and transmedia adaptation instead of print books (He et al., 2022). In other words, instead of disrupting publishers, webnovel platforms have rein-vented themselves into a new type of publisher with deep involvement and control in the entire process of digital publishing and IP exploitation in China. The key point of disparity, though, is that while print publishers make a substantial initial investment in book production and take financial risks of individual titles, webnovel platforms invest in digital infrastructure and transfer market risks to individual authors.

The digital capitalist dynamics have played a significant role in promot-ing the disruptive webnovel models in China. Cross-subsidisation is key. Just like free eBook models cross-subsidised by online advertising and platform ecosystem, webnovels are transforming from an eBook industry relying on readers' direct payment to a powerful IP engine for digital entertainment based on adaptation and IP franchising. While this offers new opportunities for China's networked writing publics, it evokes con-cerns on diminishing literary publishing into intellectual property fodder for transmedia franchising. Furthermore, the convergent developments of platformed webnovels in the context of digital capitalism are converting literary writers and readers in the book world into digital consumers for the entire platform ecosystem. The divergent visions of publishers and plat-forms already mentioned reflect deep concerns on the independence of digital publishing. Is it desirable for the networked reading publics? Will digital capitalism bring more creative liberty for webnovel writers in China's censored online sphere? Or will population-wide literary creation continue to be tamed in a digital ecosystem by both corporate and regulatory forces?

Adding to the complexity is the advent of generative AI, a cost-effective alternative to human labour on the rise. In the digital publishing industry, generative AI can both empower the writing and reading publics (Anantrasirichai & Bull, 2022) and reinforce platform power (Kenney & Zysman, 2020). Yuewen Group has already launched multimodal large language models (LLMs) called Miaobi (fantastic pen), perhaps the first in the literary publishing world. Despite the claim that 'writers will always be the protagonists' (KrASIA Connection, 2023), the potential of this model is far beyond assisting authors in creative writing. Given that Yuewen owns vast copyrighted content resources of webnovels to train AI models and the formulaic nature of genre fiction creation, Miaobi may be able to replace human labourers in various parts of the webnovel value chain. Unsurprisingly, worries about the oversupply of books and asymmetric information about quality in the AI age are comparable to some concerns in self-publishing (Hviid et al., 2019). However, bigger concerns exist in the platform's intention of exploiting the opportunities of generative AI at the cost of creators and readers, demonstrated by Amazon's arbitrary policy in filtering out AI-generated eBooks (Creamer, 2023) and Open AI's use of copyrighted literary works in training ChatGPT without right owners' permission or compensation to them (Alter & Harris, 2023).

In conclusion, the evolution of Chinese webnovels reflects parallel processes of the liberalisation, exploitation, and control of creative labour. While technological, political, and commercial factors are all powerful in shaping the webnovel system, the future relies on constructing a healthy ecology that balances the interests of authors, platforms, readers, and government, in particular, protecting individual creators' rights. While new technologies like AI and blockchain will add transformational potential, what matters is inclusive governance, addressing structural problems of labour and power in platformed self-publishing. Nevertheless, as a dynamic field with a disruptive nature, webnovels will continue to be a frontier where innovations, market dynamics, and political power collide.

4 Social Reading on WeChat and Douyin

4.1 Introduction

On social media platforms, a range of social reading activities are emerging, labelled as BookTok, BookTube, and Bookstagram (Bronwyn, 2022), where book influencers, book lovers, and participatory fans ignite passionate literary discussions and turn book reading into a viral phenomenon of digital popular culture. BookTok has become particularly a buzzword in the publishing world since 2021, with significant popularity and influence among young people, signalling how social media may transform the ways readers, content, reviewers, and authors interact (Flood, 2021). The key disruption of BookTok lies in its ability to catapult topical books on the social media sphere into bestseller lists without relying on traditional marketing channels and intermediaries, potentially revolutionising the mechanism by which book content is discovered and recommended. Parallel to the global social reading developments, on Chinese social media platforms like Douyin, WeChat, and QQ, the phenomenon of platformed social reading exhibits a similar yet different evolutionary trajectory rooted in the country's book culture, influencer economy, and media industry.

In the taxonomy-based research by Kutzner, Petzold, and Knackstedt (2019:695–686), they identify four types of social reading platforms by their characteristics, including 'manifold discussions within a bonded community', 'assessment of books to support purchase decisions', 'immediate discussions on books within a closed community', and 'hybrid discussions on books, related to sales and monetary gratification'. While China's social reading evolution encompasses initiatives in all these aspects that transform reading from a solitary act to a collective social activity, it also presents new dynamics and practices in the special context of China's platform economy. For instance, Tencent's eBook apps like QQ Read and WeChat Read allow Chinese readers to socialise their digital reading experience through deep integration with the two social media super apps QQ and WeChat. Similarly, Chinese book influencers on Douyin can not only promote bestselling books among fan communities but also sell these books directly to followers through integrated livestreaming e-commerce. As discussed in previous chapters, China's digital publishing and internet industries are highly concentrated, where a tech giant like Tencent could own the equivalence of Facebook, Amazon Kindle, Wattpad, Netflix, and Steam, and Tencent's competitor ByteDance also has deep involvement and heavy investment across webnovels, mobile reading, social media, short videos, livestreaming, and e-commerce, forming an ecosystem around Douyin (Li, 2017; Jia et al., 2022). Both Tencent and ByteDance recognise the tremendous commercial opportunities of integrating social reading with their platform ecosystem, where the networked dynamics of book communities can be further capitalised on (He, 2020).

The convergent developments of platformed social reading in China thus present a complex interplay between book influencers, reading publics, publishers, and platforms, as well as a valuable case to understand the business practices and disruptive models on the consumption side of digital publishing in the platform age. How do social media platforms foster and reshape social reading? How do QQ, WeChat, and Douyin capitalise on user participation, reader communities, and influencer popularity in their ecosystems? What power dynamics are reflected in the platformisation of social reading? This chapter addresses these questions by examining China's evolving landscape of social reading in the past two decades. Following a chronological order of the emergence of different models, it explores three major areas of social reading developments during different periods: participatory reading on eBook portals, the convergence of social reading and networking on QQ and WeChat, and the Chinese BookTok and livestreaming e-commerce on Douyin. The chapter concludes with a critical discussion on the economic value of social reading for Chinese super apps like WeChat and Douyin, as well as the implications for book publishing futures.

4.2 From Social Sharing to Participatory Reading

eBooks present both a digital form of content and a social form of reading. Just as Barnett (2015) argues, the unbinding and re-binding of books from print to digital not only take on the imagery of material books but also re-incorporate the social dimensions of material reading. In China, a range of eBook portals and digital publishing platforms are offering various initiatives that replicate and reimagine the social components of print reading, such as marginalia, book clubs, book reviews, and word-of-mouth marketing. Before delving into social reading practices on social media platforms like Douyin and WeChat, it is necessary to briefly review the development of eBook's social functions during the early years of digital publishing transformation.

Many Chinese readers' experience with eBooks started with unauthorised peer sharing on online spaces like BBS forums or social media groups, which served as the initial intermediary of digital social reading since the late 1990s. The early eBook sites like 52eBooks, rbook, and readfree gathered a large group of enthusiasts who scanned print books from libraries or personal collections and created eBooks in various formats, including txt, exe, chm, PDF, and HTML, which were usually educational materials, bestsellers, rare books, and banned books. The vibrant community of book lovers allowed eBook sharing alongside engaging discussion on book reading and eBook technology.

Along with the communal experience of social reading among eBook lovers, key social reading functions, including social highlighting, comments, sharing, and rating, were available on mainstream eBook portals and mobile reading apps in China. Readers on iReader, Duokan, and NetEase were able to socially highlight and comment at a sentence level, allowing them to share ideas with a sense of reading together in the online sphere. Among these platforms, Duokan explicitly branded itself as an eBook initiative with features of connecting readers, as conveyed by its slogan, '*Reading More Books and Making More Friends*'. Duokan's user community and co-creation model became essential for its eBook business, where eBook lovers not only discussed eBook content together but also collectively helped improve digital reading functions of the Duokan software, making it a noticeable example of user-driven innovations in China's eBook industry (Ren, 2019). Apart from eBook platforms, the Chinese social networking site Douban, launched in 2005, also has a specialised component for social book rating and reviewing, similar to Goodreads, where readers can collectively rate, review, and discuss books as well as connect with fellow readers and authors (Tian & Martin, 2013).

In the self-publishing sphere, online literature sites have emerged as another major development of social reading. As introduced in Chapter 3, online literature works, including webnovels, initially appeared on online forums featuring collective reading and writing (Hockx, 2015). During the platformisation of webnovels, social reading activities like readers' likes, votes, and comments have been gradually datafied and turned into a powerful mechanism for crowdsourced social filtering and gatekeeping on the webnovel platforms where participatory users collectively select the best stories (Shen et al., 2019). Furthermore, Chinese webnovels introduced a practical reader governance model in content creation, where active readers interacted with authors throughout their creative process, even collectively shaping the storylines, including voting for the fate of characters (Feng, 2013). As such, the confluence of self-publishing and reader engagement in the Chinese webnovel industry practically transformed the solitary activity of fiction writing and reading into a collective and co-creative experience of social storytelling.

The social reading activities on eBook portals have still been evolving. However, such innovations, that facilitate social and participatory reading largely within a particular book, are also circumscribed within the confines of the book world as a supplementary function to primary eBook consumption, enhancing reader engagement and retention while generating data for algorithmic recommendations. In the early 2010s, major eBook platforms started allowing users to log in via social media accounts such as QQ, RenRen, WeChat, Weibo, and Red. As such, readers are able to share their reading list, favourite quotes, reading progress, and reviews with their social media followers, which provides new opportunities for social media platforms to capitalise on social reading.

4.3 Convergence of Reading and Networking on QQ and WeChat

In 2010, Tencent launched its own digital reading app, QQ Read. As QQ served as a ubiquitous online personal identifier across almost all digital services and platforms in China then, this initiative, encompassing user profiles, eBooks reading, and social networking, presented significant transformative potential to harness the social media dynamics to enhance eBook business and embed digital reading into social media ecosystem. During the early 2010s, QQ Read rose in prominence in tandem with the booming Chinese webnovels, which provided a strategic opportunity for QQ to leverage its monopolistic position and extensive user base in social media to build an appealing platform for eBooks and social reading. On QQ Read, the QQ number serves as a conduit to a user's digital profile and expansive virtual identities, connecting readers, authors, and webnovel enthusiasts to socialise and interact beyond the limited social networking functions available on the specialised webnovel sites like Qidian. Despite the erstwhile anonymity of QQ networks – prior to the implementation of compulsory real name verification in social media in China – linking webnovel activity to QQ numbers had effectively nurtured interactive, communal participation in the connected social reading space. As mentioned in the previous chapter, Tencent acquired the leading webnovel company, Yuewen, in 2015, making QQ Read an essential intermediary to consolidate its position in the webnovel industry. To strengthen the connection between QQ Read and webnovel sites owned by Yuewen (like Qidian), users were allowed to sync their subscriptions and paid content for the same webnovel title across both platforms. This gives QQ Read a prestigious position as a central hub for webnovel readers, not only integrating different webnovel content sources but also connecting webnovel reading with their own social media profiles.

Apart from being one of the most popular eBook platforms, QQ Read also serves Tencent's grant strategy in building social relationships among young people based on their interests in webnovels, games, films, music, and other popular content, therefore enhancing Tencent's position in China's digital entertainment industries as a social media monopolist (Zhang, 2018). It would be safe to argue that QQ Read is an essential intermediary for Tencent's strategic direction, particularly connecting webnovels, digital reading, and QQ's social media platform. However, the business model of QQ Read remains a conventional eBook store, and priority has been given to readership growth and eBook sales. In 2023, QQ

Read even cancelled the syncing function with webnovel platforms already mentioned, as it sought to build a more independent reading platform with original and exclusive content (Mydrivers, 2023).

Compared with QQ Read, another eBook app launched by Tencent, WeChat Read, presents more innovative and disruptive practices of social reading beyond the traditional models and value proposition of eBook publishing. In Chapter 2, I introduced the innovation of WeChat Read as virtually a free eBook model based on its generous rewarding mechanism for users who participate in social reading activities. In this Chapter, I will focus more on the social reading development of WeChat Read and its integration with WeChat's social media ecosystem.

Launched in 2011, WeChat emerged in the mobile internet age, with contrasting differences from QQ, which deeply influenced the design and development of WeChat Read. WeChat is a super app for almost every Chinese individual today, largely based on users' real name information and real-world contacts, as well as the infrastructural role of WeChat connecting with various business, governmental, and entertainment systems in China (Jia et al., 2022). At the level of interpersonal communication, WeChat is a powerful tool for Chinese people to connect with families, colleagues, classmates, and friends efficiently. Moreover, there is synergy between private, semi-public, and public communications on WeChat based on semi-public social groups and public accounts, which makes WeChat a distinct environment to develop social reading initiatives like a 'knowledge club' (Potts et al., 2017), in particular, connecting people with shared interests or real-world connections through eBook reading.

When Tencent launched the second digital and social reading app, WeChat Read, Chinese publishers and industry commentators tried to interpret its intention of operating two digital reading apps, particularly given the existence and popularity of QQ Read. As already discussed, WeChat and QQ have evolved into two different social media platforms. While QQ remains a platform for anonymous or stranger networking, WeChat is largely based on users' real names and for acquaintance networking. Furthermore, WeChat and QQ are practically operated by different departments within Tencent and increasingly target different demographics: QQ is mainly for young people, while WeChat is for older users. These differences are reflected in the differentiation strategies of WeChat Read and QQ Read, as Tencent executive Zhang Rong puts it:

> The primary demographic for QQ Read is the 'post-90s' generation, characterised by their individualism, penchant for entertainment, and strong inclination towards interactivity. In catering to this group, we predominantly disseminate content that is entertaining, informative, and motivational. ... In contrast, the user base for WeChat Read skews older, and our approach here is to foster a community where users share their reading experiences. (Chen, 2017)

Apart from different demographics, the big innovations of WeChat Read compared with QQ Read are the offering of high-quality free eBooks and the deep integration between social reading and the WeChat ecosystem. Apart from what has been discussed in Chapter 2, WeChat Read employs an evolving app design to enable and facilitate such deep integration. Like other eBook apps, users can engage with eBook content at the sentence level for social highlighting and commenting on WeChat Read. However, the difference is that users can easily share their notes, highlights, and commentaries through WeChat Moment, where they can further discuss them with their contacts in the WeChat space. Additionally, through sharing one's reading lists and reading progress with real-world contacts on WeChat, the integration significantly enhances the social recommendation function of WeChat Read, potentially turning sharing into word-of-mouth book marketing. WeChat Read also has the function of Leaderboard, which tracks the time users have spent reading and turns it into a daily social competition with WeChat friends who have also opted in. As such, WeChat Read effectively enhances the gamification layer of social reading based on the acquaintance networks in the WeChat ecosystem.

Likewise, the integration of WeChat's public accounts and WeChat Read seems to be a natural move strategically, given publishers' wide adoption of public accounts to engage readers and promote books. According to the observatory data provided by China's trade press, in 2022, 132,005 articles were published by 430 WeChat public accounts in the book industry, operated by publishers and book distributors, attracting 470 million views (China Publishers, 2023a). The scale was even more expansive previously as BookTok on Douyin – a phenomenon that will be discussed in the subsequent section – caused a decline in publishers' engagement with WeChat-based social marketing (China Publishers, 2023a). Nevertheless, there is a salient endeavour to integrate WeChat's public accounts into WeChat Read, affording eBook readers book-like immersive reading experiences with the articles published on the WeChat platform. They can also take notes, highlight sentences, listen to the articles, and manage subscriptions in their personal library alongside other eBook titles. The mutual benefits of the integration are evident: readers can interact with diverse content creators, including authors, reviewers, and publishers, without leaving the app WeChat Read, and WeChat-based creators have an opportunity to connect with millions of dedicated readers.

The evolution of both QQ Read and WeChat Read reflects the continuing endeavour of Tencent, as a Chinese social media and digital entertainment giant, to exploit the social reading dynamics through a deep integration between eBook apps and social media ecosystems. The intermediary function of QQ Read connecting young people with shared interests through webnovels and the proven capabilities of WeChat Read in attracting and retaining valued demographics like urban middle-class readers both offer Tencent a vast and engaged user base for further exploitation. Moreover, the integration between social reading and social media provides valuable user and usage data across different platforms, allowing Tencent to offer more targeted products and services within and beyond the eBook field. On the other hand, both QQ Read and WeChat Read face challenges in integrating with the Tencent ecosystem, particularly balancing the sometimes-conflicting commercial interests between ecosystem-driven and eBook-centred businesses and optimising user experiences in a convergent environment of reading, networking, and connected entertainment. Furthermore, it is especially challenging for WeChat Read to develop a financially sustainable business model that goes beyond selling eBooks to readers (Zhang, 2022), particularly monetising the social reading dynamics into more tangible economic and commercial benefits for stakeholders like publishers, influencers, and authors.

4.4 BookTok with Douyin Characteristics

Unlike Tencent, Chinese social media giant ByteDance did not enter the eBook and social reading field until the late 2010s, after the commercial success of its short video platforms Douyin and TikTok. Interestingly, short video platforms emerged primarily as a competitor to book publishing as their prevalence distracts people from textual content and thus worsens the situation of public reading in China. However, Douyin and TikTok also have the unique advantages of bringing tremendous attention and internet traffic to topical books through compelling and addictive short video content and associated communications, which later evolved into a powerful social marketing channel for authors, publishers, bookstores, and book influencers. Douyin's established algorithmic content moderation and influencer economy with deep integration with e-commerce allow it to amplify the dynamics of networked social reading and significantly reshape the landscape. As such, the phenomenal BookTok offers ByteDance a prime opportunity to become a major player in China's digital publishing transformation.

According to the report released by Douyin E-Commerce (2022), over thirty million book-related videos were created and published on the platform in 2021, which increased by 43 per cent from last year, receiving nearly fifteen billion views. Douyin offers two major forms for BookTok in China: short videos and livestreaming e-commerce. For creators of short videos, Douyin has established a rewarding system that combines micro-transactions and algorithmic evaluation of content's economic value based on metrics like total views and watching time. Meanwhile, through deep integration with e-commerce, Douyin allows creators to add purchase links to their recommended books and gain commission income. Apart from short videos, Douyin's livestreaming e-commerce ecosystem plays a unique role in China's platformed and commercialised social reading developments, where top influencers and popular creators directly sell books to their followers. In 2021, 10.3 million Chinese people purchased books through Douyin livestreaming, and 49 per cent were first-time buyers, which shows great growth potential (Douyin e-Commerce, 2022; Douyin, 2023).

While Chinese knowledge influencers and famous book commentators like Fan Deng, who accumulated a reputation and built fan communities in the pre-Douyin age, are still influential, the new generation of e-commerce influencers on Douyin, like Liu Yuanyuan and Wang Fang, dominated book livestreaming (Caas Data, 2021; Xiao et al., 2023). In addition to releasing short videos regularly to keep engaging followers, these top influencers rely more on livestreaming e-commerce to generate monetary revenues. With the ease of e-commerce integration on Douyin, livestreaming, as synchronous social engagement, is powerful in converting a viewer to a buyer only through a couple of taps on the screen. The capacity of the livestreaming e-commerce profoundly reshapes the evolution of social reading and BookTok in China, as well as the book publishing business broadly, as influencers harness this advantage to not only foster a thriving community of book lovers but also transform social reading into book selling (Qu & Deng, 2023). It is worth mentioning that over 80 per cent of book sales in China occurred online in 2022, with short video and livestreaming platforms contributing 16.4 per cent of sales revenue, surpassing the share of physical bookstores at 15.3 per cent (Open Book, 2023). A notable illustration of this trend is seen in Dong Yuhui's promotion of the award-winning literary fiction *The Right Bank of the Ergun River* on Douyin livestreaming, which had sold approximately 710,000 copies within just four months, equivalent to the total sales of the novel in the seventeen years since its first edition in 2005 (Peng, 2023). As such, BookTok on Douyin is evolving into an online bookstore where influencers work as booksellers.

It is thus understandable that perhaps, unlike their Western colleagues, Chinese publishers and book institutions are very actively participating in BookTok. Over 300 state-owned publishing houses and over 10,000 publishing institutions, including private book companies, book wholesalers, and bookstores, have official accounts on Douyin (Douyin e-Commerce, 2022). One pressing issue pushing these organisations to do book livestreaming or create BookTok content themselves is the heavy discounts they have to offer Douyin's top influencers in livestreaming e-commerce. Due to their scale and dominance, these influencers usually demand publishers to give them heavy discounts on their books, like other types of commodities sold on the platform, which, however, as a new type of distribution dominance, is threatening the sustainability of book business (Huang, 2021). Another driving force was China's unique public health regulations during the pandemic, particularly the restrictive and frequent lockdowns in major cities, which forced publishers and bookstores to develop livestreaming e-commerce and online retailing to sell books (The Paper, 2020).

While BookTok and livestreaming offer publishers and bookstores new opportunities to directly engage vast readers, achieving commercial success in this digital venture remains a challenge. As with WeChat-based social marketing, there is a significant polarisation in publishers' performance in BookTok and livestreaming (Gao & Duan, 2021). Despite a few leading publishers like CITIC Press achieving notable success in BookTok (China Publishers, 2023b), the majority face limitations in audience reach and engagement due to insufficient fan base accumulation, lack of engaging and interactive content, varying levels of commitment and capabilities in social media marketing, and heavy reliance on celebrity endorsements and low-price strategies (Gao & Duan, 2021). The publishers' difficulty is unsurprising also due to the nature of algorithm-driven content moderation on Douyin, which prioritises the relevance and appeal of content instead of the official authority or number of followers the creators have (Su, 2023), making it more challenging for publishing institutions to secure popularity in Douyin's BookTok than on other platforms.

Douyin's distributed algorithm also contributes to a gradual trend where mid-tier or micro-influencers, as well as individual book enthusiasts, are becoming more fundamental than publishers and macro-influencers in BookTok, as the creators with 10,000 to three million followers contributed to over 70 per cent of total book sales on Douyin e-Commerce (Douyin e-Commerce, 2022). Unlike high-profile influencers, micro-influencers and ordinary book lovers have different content styles and cultural practices of BookTok, focusing on sharing personal reading experiences as relatable fellow book lovers rather than expert educators (Bronwyn, 2022). Accordingly, their public image is shifting from an authoritative, directive mentor, typically a senior male intellectual, to easy-going ordinary people simply sharing knowledge with connected communities. This is especially true given that 71 per cent of BookTok participants on Douyin are female (Douyin e-Commerce, 2022), among whom books and reading constitute an exceptionally beloved subject matter for discussion. Educated young mothers are a particularly active demographic group who manage to transform their passion for reading into an engaging outreach activity on social media as micro-influencers on BookTok (Cheng, 2020). This shift contributes to the humanisation of book recommendations with high para-social relationships (Yang & Ha, 2021) and the formation of a trusted communal environment for social reading. Furthermore, these creators typically focus on the areas relating to their background or expertise, and the content is usually tailored to like-minded followers, addressing their specific knowledge demands, anxiety, and problems in the specialist area.

As such, Douyin-based BookTok presents a distributed power structure of book influencers and, thus, a process of democratisation in book reviews and recommendations, which may potentially alter the mechanism of taste-making and gatekeeping in the book publishing world broadly and pro-foundly. Based on diverse social reading communities, it is unsurprising that China's BookTok and book livestreaming cover a broader range of book titles. Regarding internet traffic, literary books received the most views, followed by history, life guides, popular science, and poetry on Douyin in 2023 (Douyin, 2023). However, when it comes to book sales in livestreaming e-commerce, Children's books lead at 36 per cent, followed by educational books at 11 per cent, and self-help books at 9 per cent in 2022 (Douyin e-Commerce, 2022). This diverse pattern may differ from Western BookTok developments that usually focus on young adult and popular literature (Dezuanni et al., 2022).

While this is a testament to the power of Douyin in shaping reading trends and promoting bestselling books, their social reading practice faces challenges and controversies. Douyin unavoidably faces competition from different social media platforms in the field, including WeChat and Weibo, and emerging platforms like Bilibili. As 'an iconic brand and a leading video community for young generations in China' with 96.5 million average daily active users (Bilibili, 2023), Bilibili's emphasis on participatory creation and subcultures contrasts with Douyin's com-mercially formulaic content style. Bilibili is especially known for the 'bullet curtain' commentary system, allowing real-time audience discus-sion and reaction within videos. The unique communal and participatory model of social interaction on Bilibili, as well as its historical connection with Chinese anime and subculture communities (Wang, 2022), makes it advantageous in leveraging grassroots creativity to build a youth-oriented social reading ecosystem, competing with Douyin's more commercialised and mainstream one.

More profound challenges and controversy lie in trust and authenticity in the social recommendation of books on Douyin. Parallel to the rise of BookTok is the erosion of public trust in experts, including both the official intellectuals based at universities or public institutions and the market-driven knowledge influencers and public intellectuals (Benkler et al., 2018; Shao & Ieong, 2022). While Chinese BookTok is shifting away from expert influencers lecturing about broad topics towards empowering micro-influencers and niche communities, the democratising and diversifying process still revolves around the authenticity of book reviews. The line between a genuine endorsement by book lovers and intentional promotions driven by commercial motivations should be distinct. Furthermore, there is a growing risk of trivialising or tabloidising books due to the pressure to produce viral content, turning even peer-to-peer sharing of reading experiences, favourite quotes, and personal views into a public display, which thus contributes to a performance culture in the digital book world. Douyin's powerful algorithm is also a double-edged sword, which can both make ordinary books a viral topic on social media and limit the diversity of books promoted, restricting readers' exposure to a wide range of bookish content (Zukin, 2022). In short, despite the commercial success and cultural influence of Douyin-based BookTok, more innovations and efforts are required to boost a healthy social reading culture based on the genuine pleasure of reading and intellectual discovery and trusted peer recommendations.

4.5 How Super Apps Reshape Social Reading

China's social reading evolution brings direct benefits and opportunities to readers and publishers, as participatory readers could engage in social reading activities to share bookish experiences and connect with like-minded communities, and publishers could embed social functions to optimise digital reading experiences and attract and retain readers. However, the evolution of social reading also involves a process of platformisation where platform companies leverage their monopolist position as infrastructural intermediaries to capitalise on social reading in their ecosystems. Just like free eBook apps and platformed webnovels discussed in previous chapters, the platformisation of social reading results in the expansion of big tech companies into the book field. Social reading thus provides another snapshot of the disruptive process where super apps like QQ, WeChat, and Douyin restructure the book publishing value chain and growingly achieve dominance.

Despite the appreciation of social marketing opportunities with Douyin and WeChat, Chinese publishers are concerned about the dominance of platformed social reading in book distribution (Huang, 2021). This results in growing tension between publishers and social media platforms, with complaints about the free eBook offerings of WeChat Read and the heavy discounts given to Douyin e-commerce vendors, as mentioned previously. Adding to the controversy is that many top influencers on Douyin's livestreaming e-commerce are not book specialists or genuine book lovers at all. Rather than recommending good books to readers, they are more motivated by the discounts and profits, resulting in viewers being attracted merely by low prices (Chen, 2022). For the long term, BookTok-driven book sales through an influencer economy and discounted prices may overdraw the future potential of book demands and thus threaten the sustainability of book publishing. In 2022, while BookTok and livestreaming e-commerce led to a surge in book sales based on Douyin, it coincided with a decline in the total revenue in China's book industry (Open Book, 2023).

Publishers' deeper concern with WeChat and Douyin lies in the distribution of economic values in terms of user co-creation, user data, and internet traffic generated through free eBook reading. In the context of Douyin BookTok, for instance, while topical books and star authors help bring attention and internet traffic to the social media ecosystem, not all these dynamics have been converted into book sales or tangible benefits for publishers. There is thus a risk of books becoming merely a commodity sold with heavy discounts on e-commerce platforms or, even worse, a topical and eye-catching subject that may drive social marketing revenue growth in other sectors.

From the platform perspective, the rapid growth and vast potential of China's social reading market presents unprecedented commercial opportunities. Established players such as Tencent can incorporate social networking features into apps like QQ Read and WeChat Read and further connect social reading with platformed webnovels, online games, video streaming, and transmedia IP franchising in a pan-entertainment ecosystem. New entrants like ByteDance are actively expanding in the field through acquisition, investment, and partnership to challenge Tencent's dominance. For instance, ByteDance invested RMB 1.1 billion (USD 150 million) in iReader, making it the third-largest shareholder (Yu, 2020), and formed a strategic partnership with another leading eBook company, ChineseAll (Sohu, 2021). Meanwhile, as discussed in previous chapters, ByteDance is building its own entertainment ecosystem around Douyin through the development of ad-supported free eBooks and mini-dramas, where Douyin BookTok becomes a strategic asset for engaging readers and collaborating with publishers.

As such, social reading is a battlefield between super apps like WeChat and Douyin and between the entertainment ecosystems of Tencent and ByteDance. Adding to the increasingly fierce battle are other competing forces like Bilibili, Zhihu, and Douban. In such a competitive market environment where Tencent's monopolist advantage is being challenged, publishers may benefit from more options and pathways for collaborating with tech platforms. However, in the ecosystem competition, tech giants are also actively expanding their reach in the publishing industry, operating in content production, acquisition, distribution, franchising, and reader engagement. This is exemplified by their deep involvement in the disruptive areas of free eBooks, self-publishing, and social reading, examined throughout this Element. All these evolutionary developments will facilitate the process of integrating digital publishing and reading into the platform ecosystems of super apps, which, however, may further empower the platforms while marginalising traditional publishers. This will result in both opportunities and uncertainties for book communities. In the next chapter, I will continue the discussion on the impact of super apps and large platforms in light of emerging technologies such as generative AI, blockchain, and metaverse, and conclude the Element with a post-eBook vision of publishing futures. .

5 Conclusion: Disruptions and eBooks Futures

5.1 Global Implications of China's eBook Evolution

An inquiry throughout this Element is whether China's digital publishing developments present a fundamentally different 'other' that requires interpretation to understand or an alternative model that may inspire digital publishing futures globally. China is one of the world's largest and oldest book markets, with a vast economic scale and thousands of years of publishing history. However, due to the linguistic base of Chinese language publications and government control over market entry, China often exists as a separate system from the book world concentrated in North America and Europe, unfamiliar from a Western perspective. Over the past decades, the pace of digital transformation and upgrading of China's book sector has been astonishing, largely led by Chinese tech giants like Tencent, ByteDance, and Baidu instead of traditional publishers. Parallel to the industrial transformation is the governmental investment in digital infrastructures and strict internet regulations, both of which are Chinese characteristics, uniquely reshaping the evolution of eBooks in the country.

While recognising the distinctiveness of China's digital publishing landscape, we should also acknowledge the global relevance of its eBook innovations as well as their impacts and challenges, studying them with an open mind. As shown in the case study chapters, a range of components of China's eBook models resonate with global digital trends, and so do the concerns of major stakeholders facing an increasingly disruptive and uncertain digital environment in the platform age. The value of disruptive eBook innovations in China in offering affordable and accessible content to large populations, particularly those excluded or disadvantaged in print publishing, may find similar developments in other emerging markets like India, South America, and Southeast Asia (Gudinavičius & Grigas, 2022; Rose, 2022). Likewise, the concentrated power of platform companies in China, as well as their powerful influence in reshaping the book business, reading cultures, and publishing ecosystems, is undeniably a shared concern in the global publishing community (Anderson, 2020; Johnson, 2021). Despite the different political, linguistic, and social contexts, China offers an advanced glimpse into the complexity of eBook practices and an alternative vision illuminating possible trajectories for global digital publishing evolution.

Apart from the radical disruptions and transformative changes analysed in this Element, mostly led by digital platforms, the intricate yet dynamic co-evolution between the emerging and established systems is also a feature of China's eBook evolution. As mentioned in Chapter 1, the Chinese stakeholders generally hold an open attitude towards disruptive innovations in digital publishing and are increasingly willing to collaborate with digital platforms under the shared umbrella vision of 'internet plus publishing'. There is a dynamic interplay between continuity and change in the convergent and co-evolutional developments, which indicates both the transformative power of disruptive models and the endurance of publishing principles, evidenced by the rejuvenation of traditional publishing components in disruptive initiatives. For instance, eBook start-up Duokan is ambitious in replicating the pleasure of print reading in their eBook apps; webnovel platforms reinstalled editorial roles to mentor online writers and assume gatekeeping functions; and the conventional paid eBook models returned on WeChat Read and China Mobile Reading Base after their rapid market expansion driven by free content offering. In the meantime, facing eBook disruptions, Chinese publishers' coping strategies and adaptive innovations in BookTok and social marketing provide a snapshot of their efforts in balancing digital opportunities and publishing independence. All of these empirical cases are valuable for reimagining the publishing business in a platform economy and revisiting key issues such as digital labour, power structures, and platform governance in the digital publishing world.

Furthermore, this Element pays special attention to the competition between tech platforms in digital publishing ecosystems. While Chinese tech giants endeavour to integrate digital reading into their own platform business, it has brought the book world into the competition between expansive internet ecosystems. In this Element, the ecosystem war between Tencent, ByteDance, and other tech giants is visible and influential in all three disruptive areas examined. In the market of ad-supported free eBooks, ByteDance challenges Tencent's dominance in webnovels based on subscription models. Webnovel adaptations and IP franchising have also become a battlefield where Tencent's pan-entertainment strategy leverages top-tier webnovel IPs while Douyin's investments in mini-dramas capitalise on middle-tier titles. The evolution of social reading ultimately leads to direct competition between the WeChat and Douyin ecosystems, where they compete for a dominant position in the extended book value chain, driven by the dynamics of micro-influencers, BookTok communities, and livestreaming e-commerce. Undeniably, the deep involvement of tech giants in eBook evolution may not be replicable in other contexts due to China's unique regulatory and industrial environment, in particular, its relatively relaxed platform regulations in cross-media ownership and concentration. However, from a global perspective, it provides a valuable perspective on the tensions among tech giants in the evolution of platformed digital publishing.

5.2 The Post-eBook Age and Beyond

The Chinese eBook practices and discourses reflect a consistent yet ambitious vision of digital publishing, crossing the conventional boundaries of book formats, distribution channels, reading markets, and publishing economy, which is thus defined broadly as a digital content industry or digital creative industry (Flew et al., 2019; Zhang et al., 2021). China's ambition of harnessing digital modernisation to catch up with the West in digital publishing (Liu, 2008) has led to fewer restrictions but more space for radical innovations. Furthermore, as disruptive forces normally emerge outside the publishing domain in China, publisher and non-publisher entities have formed two sharply different groups in digital publishing. Being called 'the wolves at the door' by publishers, digital initiatives, without the constraints of traditional systems, were able to embrace disruptive ideas to develop eBook business in fundamentally different ways, signifying a radical break from traditional models, sometimes along with a progressive agenda of evolution. As demonstrated in many cases in this Element, eBook evolution in China has arguably moved beyond the conventional eBook paradigm exemplified by Amazon Kindle.

I thus employ a post-eBook perspective to conceptualise the paradigm shift that occurred along with continuing evolutionary changes in China. Specifically, parallel to the internet evolution broadly, I categorise three evolutionary stages with overlaps, where a big shift of publishing models occurred in China, transforming the business logic and cultures of eBooks. The Web 2.0 age, grounded in the notion of participatory publishing and a blurred line between professional and amateur creators, saw the rise of webnovels as not only a Chinese counterpart of global self-publishing and social authoring (Ramdarshan Bold, 2018) but also a vast and highly industrialised alternative system largely displacing the Chinese traditional literary publishing. Platformisation (Van Dijck et al., 2018) led to the next big shift, in particular, the dominance of digital platforms in mediating digital publishing, writing, and reading, exemplified by webnovel platforms like Qidian, digital reading apps like QQ Read, and mobile reading platforms like China Mobile Reading Base. These platforms profoundly changed the understanding and practice of the publishing business through data-driven models, algorithmic content moderation, network effects, and infrastructural intermediation (Srnicek, 2016). Along with platformisation, Chinese tech giants also develop their own platform ecosystems through cross-platform integration and transmedia convergence (Ren, 2022), where digital reading is deeply integrated with social media, online advertising, and e-commerce, based on super apps like WeChat and Douyin. The ecosystem paradigm signifies the value reproposition of digital publishing and reading in datafication, internet traffic, and e-commerce conversion. All of these values, beyond the content industry, contribute to the sustainability, competitiveness, and monopoly of tech giants' platform ecosystems.

The post-eBook evolution will continue with emerging technologies like generative AI. The advent of ChatGPT, as well as the population-wide access to powerful AI applications, is unprecedentedly transforming the production, discovery, distribution, and consumption of eBooks. I have introduced Miaobi, the LLM launched by Yuewen Group, in Chapter 3. Another noticeable development is the Magic Media Large Model, launched by the Chinese publishing technology monopolist Founder, along with an AI-based toolkit, to automate publishing processes from content creation to digital marketing (Yi, 2023). Apart from LLMs, Chinese digital publishing companies have also applied AI technologies in the development of interactive reading products. Even before the rise of ChatGPT, the 'IP awakening plan' of Yuewen in 2019, in collaboration with Microsoft's Xiaoice Avatar Framework, already used AI and virtual reality to give 'life' to 100 male protagonists of popular webnovels, allowing female readers to intimately interact with these virtual companions to develop exclusive storylines and conversations (Hua, 2019). More recently, Xiaorui, a 'digital human' product, has been adopted by over twenty publishers, serving as an interactive reading assistant that humanises reader interface and digital reading based on the database of over a million publications (Sohu, 2023). The rapid development of industry-specific LLM reflects the proactive efforts of Chinese digital publishing monopolists in this emerging field, where they leverage the ownership and control of Chinese language content resources to build competitive advantages (Ouyang, 2023). However, the monopolist positions of Chinese tech giants, as the owners of copyrighted content, technological infrastructures, and commercial ecosystems, may lead to unethical applications of AI technologies, as well as devaluation and disempowerment of human creativity in the digital publishing field.

Generative AI is only one of the emerging technologies that are transforming digital publishing, alongside blockchain, mixed realities, cloud computing, 5 G, and many others. The monopolist position of tech giants undeniably facilitates deep integration across these technological territories. While this has opened new opportunities for readers, authors, and publishers to revolutionise digital publishing and reading to the next level, it unavoidably strengthens the platform's power further. Nowadays, emergent tech-driven initiatives in digital publishing, like digital collections, virtual companions, interactive reading, and mixed reality eBooks, largely rely on the digital infrastructures provided by platform companies. Apart from tech giants, the government will play a significant role in shaping the next wave of disruptive innovations in the post-eBook era. China's centralised approach to distributed technologies, such as blockchain, and potentially AI development in the near future, coupled with stringent regulations and censorship, means that their influence should not be underestimated.

5.3 Conclusion

The eBook evolution in China has significantly expanded the boundaries of the publishing business beyond a small 'book world', opening up new opportunities through disruptive technologies and platform ecosystems.

This becomes especially meaningful when the decline of reading among young people becomes a global trend in today's multiscreen, transmedia, and entertainment-centric digital environment, particularly for print publications (Clark et al., 2023; Institute for Chinese Press and Publication, 2023). The potential crisis or transformation of reading necessitates a new approach to engage young readers, embracing digital dynamics in book cultures.

While disruption and uncertainty are the new normal, the independence and resilience of book publishing becomes more important than ever. China's eBook evolution, where different models coexist, compete, and coevolve, reflects various contesting values underpinning the innovations, including, but not limited to, open versus closed, centralisation versus decentralisation, privacy versus surveillance, transparency versus black box, profit-driven versus socially conscious, and platform versus community. There is certainly a disparity between what is held among publishing communities and what is valued by tech companies. However, is it still desirable to endure the values that have underpinned the book world for centuries? How can publishing communities maintain their status and influence amidst the dominance of tech giants' platform ecosystems? And how can disruptive innovations be used to develop an open-source, decentralised, or communal ecosystem for digital publishing as an alternative to corporate platforms?

The Chinese eBook evolution has yet to offer a clear vision on these big questions, but the ambitious experiments have never been absent. Today's publishing world faces great uncertainty stemming from disruptive technologies, economic volatility, and geopolitical tensions, which publishing communities across the world must grapple with. China will continue to be a powerhouse in digital publishing, as well as an experimental playground for new ideas.

References

Alter, A. & Harris, E. A. (2023). 'Franzen, Grisham and Other Prominent Authors Sue OpenAI', *The New York Times*, 20 September, www.nytimes.com/2023/09/20/books/authors-openai-lawsuit-chatgpt-copyright.html. Accessed 20 October 2023.

Anantrasirichai, N. & Bull, D. (2022). 'Artificial Intelligence in the Creative Industries: A Review', *Artificial Intelligence Review*, 55(1), pp. 589–656. https://doi.org/10.1007/s10462-021-10039-7.

Anderson, P. (2020). 'US Publishers, Authors, Booksellers Call Out Amazon's "Concentrated Power"', *Publishing Perspectives*, 17 August, https://publishingperspectives.com/2020/08/us-publishers-authors-booksellers-call-out-amazons-concentrated-power-in-the-book-market/. Accessed 5 June 2021.

Araman, V. F. & Popescu, I. (2010). 'Media Revenue Management with Audience Uncertainty: Balancing Upfront and Spot Market Sales', *Manufacturing & Service Operations Management*, 12(2), pp. 190–212. https://doi.org/10.1287/msom.1090.0262.

Bai, R. (2019). 'Refashioning Chinese Television through Digital Fun', in S. Shimpach (ed.) *The Routledge Companion to Global Television*. Oxfordshire: Routledge, pp. 359–370.

Banet-Weiser S. (2011). 'Branding the Post-feminist Self: Girls' Video Production and YouTube', in Kearney CK (ed.) *Mediated Girlhoods: New Explorations of Girls' Media Culture*. New York: Peter Lang Publishing, pp. 277–294.

Barnett, T. (2015). 'Platforms for Social Reading: The Material Book's Return', *Scholarly and Research Communication*, 6(4), pp. 1–23. https://doi.org/10.22230/src.2015v6n4a211.

Bartholomeusz, S. (2022). '"Barbaric Growth": China Tightens Grip on Engine that Powers Its Economy', *The Sydney Morning Herald*, 9 February, www.smh.com.au/business/the-economy/barbaric-growth-china-looks-to-tighten-grip-on-engine-that-powers-its-economy-20220209-p59uxw.html. Accessed 3 October 2023.

Benkler, Y., Faris, R., & Roberts, H. (2018). *Network Propaganda: Manipulation, Disinformation, and Radicalization in American Politics*. Oxford: Oxford University Press.

Bhaskar, M. (2016). *Curation: The Power of Selection in a World of Excess*. London: Little, Brown Book Group.

Bhaskar, M. (2020). 'AI and Publishing: What Next?', *Logos*, 31(3), pp. 13–19. https://doi.org/10.1163/18784712-03103003.

Bilibili, (2023). *Bilibili Inc. Announces Second Quarter 2023 Financial Results*, 17 August, https://tools.eurolandir.com/tools/PressReleases/GetPressRelease/?ID=4367425&lang=en-GB&companycode=services. Accessed 3 October 2023.

Bronwyn, R. (2022). 'Social Reading Cultures on BookTube, Bookstagram, and BookTok', *Synergy*, 20(1). https://slav.vic.edu.au/index.php/Synergy/article/view/597/592.

Caas Data (2021). *Who Is No. 1 in Book Livestreaming E-Commerce?* 26 September, https://36kr.com/p/1415359050651273. Accessed 25 October 2023.

CADPA (2021). *2020 Annual Report of Digital Reading in China*. Beijing: China Audio-video and Digital.

Chen, A. (2020). 'Authors Strike to Protest Alleged IP Abuse by Tencent-Backed China Literature', *PingWest*, 11 May, https://en.pingwest.com/a/6633. Accessed 11 September 2023.

Chen, J. (2017). *Internet Giants Lay Out Plans for the Mass Reading Market*, 19 June, http://tech.china.com.cn/internet/20170609/301474.shtml. Accessed 8 September 2023.

Chen, M. (2022). *In-Depth Report on Yuewen Group (0772. HK) – The Path of Advancement for the Super IP Factory*. Beijing: Sealand Securities, p. 85.

Chen, X. (2011). '2010: The Turning Point for Chinese Book Publishing Industry', *Publishing Research Quarterly*, 27(1), pp. 76–82. https://doi.org/10.1007/s12109-011-9203-x.

Chen, X. (2022). 'When Books Meet Live Streaming', *Guang Ming Daily*, 5 July. http://cul.china.com.cn/2022-07/05/content_42025271.htm. Accessed 30 October 2023.

Cheng, C. (2020). *Song Yu | Full-Time Mom on Douyin, Sharing a Unique Parenting Approach*, 14 October, www.dsb.cn/129275.html. Accessed 25 October 2023.

Chi, H. (2013). 'The Largest E-Book Piracy Case in the Country Has Been Busted', *China News*, 27 July, www.chinanews.com.cn/cul/2013/07-27/5091954.shtml. Accessed 18 August 2023.

China Literature (2018). *China Literature Limited 2017 Annual Report*. https://ir-1253177085.cos.ap-hongkong.myqcloud.com/investment/20200220/5e4e01fb1780c.pdf. Accessed 8 September 2023.

China Literature (2022). *China Literature Limited 2021 Annual Report*. Hong Kong: China Literature. https://ir-1253177085.cos.ap-hongkong.myqcloud.com/investment/20220419/625e4587b8e1d.pdf. Accessed 6 September 2023.

China Literature (2023). *China Literature Limited 2022 Annual Report*. Hong Kong: China Literature. https://ir-1253177085.cos.ap-hongkong.myqcloud.com/investment/20230418/643e7c5325696.pdf. Accessed 6 September 2023.

China Publishers (2023a). *2022 Book Industry WeChat Official Account Annual List | Is the Era of Graphics and Texts Coming to an End?* 28 January, www.sohu.com/a/635029538_121123863. Accessed 13 August 2023.

China Publishers (2023b). *Dialogue with Fang Xi: CITIC Publishing Must Be Profitable with Self-Broadcasting, while Long Videos Lay the Path for the Future*, 13 March, www.sohu.com/a/653609965_121123863. Accessed 2 October 2023.

Chinese Academy of Social Sciences (2022). *2021 Report on the Development of Chinese Online Literature*. Beijing: Chinese Academy of Social Sciences.

Chinese Academy of Social Sciences (2023). *2022 Report on the Development of Chinese Online Literature*. Beijing: Chinese Academy of Social Sciences.

Christensen, C., McDonald, R., Altman, E., & Palmer, J. (2018). 'Disruptive Innovation: An Intellectual History and Directions for Future Research', *Journal of Management Studies*, 55(7), pp. 1043–1078. https://doi.org/10.1111/joms.12349.

Clark, C., Picton, I., & Galway, M. (2023). *Children and Young People's Reading Trends in 2023*. London: National Literacy Trust. https://nlt.cdn.ngo/media/documents/Reading_trends_2023.pdf. Accessed 15 October 2023.

Clark, P. (1984). *Popular Chinese Literature and Performing Arts in the People's Republic of China, 1949–1979*. Oakland: University of California Press.

Cloudary Corporation (2012). *Amendment No.8 to Form F-1*, 7 May, www.sec.gov/Archives/edgar/data/1518239/000119312512214147/d208939df1a.htm. Accessed 6 September 2023.

CNNIC (2019). *The 44th China Statistical Report on Internet Development*. Beijing: CNNIC.

Creamer, E. (2023). 'Self-Publishers Must Declare if Content Sold on Amazon's Site Is AI-Generated', *The Guardian*, 11 September, www.theguardian.com/books/2023/sep/11/self-publishers-must-declare-if-content-sold-on-amazons-site-is-ai-generated. Accessed 20 October 2023.

Cui, H. (2022). *Annual Report on Digital Publishing Industry in China: 2021–2022*. Beijing: China Book Press.

Deng, W. (2019). 'Media Industry: Detailed Comparison of Midu, Lianshang, and Feidu to Understand the Characteristics and Future of the Free Reading Model', *Sina Finance*, 3 April, http://stock.finance.sina.com.cn/stock/go.php/Report_Show/kind/search/rptid/607627708471/index.phtml. Accessed 20 August 2023.

Dezuanni, M., Reddan, B., Rutherford, L., & Schoonens, A. (2022). 'Selfies and Shelfies on #bookstagram and #booktok – Social Media and the Mediation of Australian Teen Reading', *Learning, Media and Technology*, 47(3), pp. 355–372. https://doi.org/10.1080/17439884.2022.2068575.

Ding, T. (2021). *Online Reading APP, WeChat Reading and Tomato Novels Are Undercurrents*, 11 June, www.jiemian.com/article/6223345.html. Accessed 13 August 2023.

Domon, K., Melcarne, A., & Ramello, G. B. (2019). Digital Piracy in Asian Countries. *Journal of Industrial and Business Economics*, 46(1), pp. 117–135. https://doi.org/10.1007/s40812-019-00111-3.

DoNews (2020). 'Can ByteDance Realise the Dream of Pan-Entertainment?', *Huxiu*, 5 August, www.huxiu.com/article/373609.html. Accessed 13 August 2023.

Dong, S. & Wu, S. (2017). *Sprawling and Low-Quality Content, Fragmented Reading, Rampant Plagiarism: Three Hidden Concerns Amplified by Digital Reading*, 11 May, www.xinhuanet.com/politics/2017-05/11/c_1120952308.htm. Accessed 5 October 2023.

Douyin (2023). *2023 Report on the Ecosystem of Douyin Book Reading*. Beijing: Douyin Group.

Douyin e-Commerce (2022). *Report on the Development of the Book Industry in Douyin E-Commerce*. Beijing: Douyin Group.

Driscoll, B., Fletcher, L., Wilkins, K., & Carter, D. (2018). 'The Publishing Ecosystems of Contemporary Australian Genre Fiction', *Creative Industries Journal*, 11(2), pp. 203–221. https://doi.org/10.1080/17510694.2018.1480851.

Einarsson, K., Taylor, J., Mendoza-Sepulveda, N., & Salama, M. (2023). 'The International Publishers Association Freedom to Publish Committee – Challenges and Accomplishments', *Publishing Research Quarterly*, 39(1), pp. 34–46. https://doi.org/10.1007/s12109-022-09931-z.

Feng, J. (2013). *Romancing the Internet: Producing and Consuming Chinese Web Romance*. Leiden: Brill.

Filloux, F. (2012). 'eBooks: The Giant Disruption', *The Guardian*, 27 February, www.theguardian.com/technology/2012/feb/27/ebooks-giant-disruption-publishing. Accessed 29 May 2021.

Flew, T. (2021). *Regulating Platforms*. Cambridge, UK: Polity Press.

Flew, X., Ren, X., & Wang, Y. (2019). 'Creative Industries in China: The Digital Turn', in S. Cunningham & T. Flew (eds.) *A Research Agenda for Creative Industries*. Cheltenham, UK: Edward Elgar, pp. 164–178.

Flood, A. (2021). 'The Rise of BookTok: Meet the Teen Influencers Pushing Books Up the Charts', *The Guardian*, 25 June. www.theguardian.com/books/2021/jun/25/the-rise-of-booktok-meet-the-teen-influencers-pushing-books-up-the-charts. Accessed 24 October 2023.

Frater, P. (2018). 'Inside Alibaba and Tencent's Plans for World Media Domination', *Variety*, 3 May. https://variety.com/2018/biz/asia/alibaba-tencent-china-1202795583/. Accessed 17 October 2023.

Gao, H. & Duan, J. (2021). 'Livestream Marketing of Chinese Publishing Enterprises: Current Status, Issues, and Countermeasures – Empirical Analysis Based on Taobao Livestreaming', *China Editor*, (5). www.sohu.com/a/471047365_121123682. Accessed 2 October 2023.

Gilbert, R. J. (2015). 'E-Books: A Tale of Digital Disruption', *Journal of Economic Perspectives*, 29(3), pp. 165–184. https://doi.org/10.1257/jep.29.3.165.

Global Times (2020). 'Controversial Contract of China's Online Literature Platform Causes a Stir', *Global Times*, 4 May, www.globaltimes.cn/content/1187375.shtml. Accessed 11 September 2023.

Goh, B. (2022). *Amazon to Pull Kindle Out of China, Other Businesses to Remain*, 2 June, https://money.usnews.com/investing/news/articles/2022-06-02/amazon-says-will-shut-kindle-bookstore-in-china-next-year. Accessed 3 October 2023.

Graziani, T. (2018). 'Chinese Mobile eBook Market Is Booming', *WalktheChat*, 27 October. https://walkthechat.com/chinese-mobile-ebook-market-is-booming/. Accessed 19 August 2023.

Gudinavičius, A. & Grigas, V. (2022). 'Two Decades of E-Book Publishing in a Small Language Market: Publishers Lag Behind Pirates', *Publishing Research Quarterly*, 38(3), pp. 490–502. https://doi.org/10.1007/s12109-022-09894-1.

Han, R. & Huang, S. (2019). 'The De-politicization of Internet Literature in China', *Australian Journal of Basic and Applied Sciences* [Preprint]. https://doi.org/10.22587/ajbas.2019.13.8.16.

Hao, Z., Wei, Y., & Xu, S. (2008). 'Latest Trends of Reading in China', *Publishing Research Quarterly*, 24(1), pp. 4–8. https://doi.org/10.1007/s12109-008-9065-z.

He, H. (2020). *Optimising during Adjustment, Moving towards Mainstream Development*, 20 January, https://m.aapplewood.com/n1/2020/0120/c404027-31556551.html. Accessed 11 September 2023.

He, H. (2022). 'Passionately Depicting the New Era Is the Mission to Which Web Literature Is Bound', *CCTV*, 16 April, https://news.cctv.com/2022/04/16/ARTIwgRfUMa6uXsM2KaT45z8220416.shtml. Accessed 30 August 2023.

He, P. (2020). 'Why Are Big Factories Doing Book Reading Business?', *JMedia Official Account*, 24 October, www.jiemian.com/article/5163237.html. Accessed 13 August 2023.

He, W., Lin, L., & Fung, A. (2022). 'Online Fiction Writers, Labor, and Cultural Economy', *Global Media and China*, 7(2), pp. 169–182. https://doi.org/10.1177/20594364221105643.

Hepp, A., Schmitz, A., & Schneider, N. (2023). 'Afterlives of the Californian Ideology| Afterlives of the Californian Ideology: Tech Movements, Pioneer Communities, and Imaginaries of Digital Futures – Introduction', *International Journal of Communication*, 17(0), p. 19.

Hepu (n.d.). 'Free Reading App, I Only Keep These Two', *Zhihu Column*. https://zhuanlan.zhihu.com/p/53727366. Accessed 12 August 2023.

Hernández, J. C. & Zhang, A. (2018). 'Writer of Erotic Novels in China Is Jailed for Producing Gay Pornography', *The New York Times*, 19 November. www.nytimes.com/2018/11/19/world/asia/tianyi-china-erotic-novels-prison.html. Accessed 11 September 2023.

Heyman, S. (2015). 'Taxes on Digital Books Are Called Unfair', *The New York Times*, 29 July. www.nytimes.com/2015/07/30/arts/international/taxes-on-digital-books-are-called-unfair.html. Accessed 3 October 2023.

Hockx, M. (2015). *Internet Literature in China*. New York: Columbia University Press.

Hu, H. (2020). 'The Way of Survival: Labour Differentiation and Subjective Practices among Online Literature Authors', *China Youth Research*, (12). www.sohu.com/a/436149534_690232. Accessed 9 September 2023.

Hu, Y. (2023). *Yuewen Will Change CEOs after Three Years: What Will Cheng Wu Leave Behind? What Will Hou Xiaonan Bring?* 9 May, https://m.jiemian.com/article/9372062.html. Accessed 13 August 2023.

Hua, Z. (2019). *The 'IP Awakening Plan' Is Here! Want to Date a Web Novel Male Lead? Choose From 100 Novels' Male Leads!*, 25 September, www.sohu.com/a/343361055_120046696#google_vignette. Accessed 15 October 2023.

Huang, H. (2021). *Setting Aside Emotions, How Should the Publishing Industry Rationally Perceive This Phenomenon of Live Broadcasts Exceeding One Hundred Million in Book Sales?* 2 October, https://m.thepaper.cn/newsDetail_forward_14743146. Accessed 2 October 2023.

Huang, X. & Hao, T. (2014). 'System of Digital Publishing Policies and Regulations in China', *Library Hi Tech*, 32(3), pp. 397–408. https://doi.org/10.1108/LHT-06-2013-0082.

Hutchinson, J. (2023). *Digital Intermediation: Unseen Infrastructure for Cultural Production*. London: Routledge.

Hviid, M., Izquierdo-Sanchez, S., & Jacques, S. (2019). 'From Publishers to Self-Publishing: Disruptive Effects in the Book Industry', *International Journal of the Economics of Business*, 26(3), pp. 355–381. https://doi.org/10.1080/13571516.2019.1611198.

iFeng (2010). 'China Mobile's Mobile Reading Goes Public, Plans Not to Make a Profit for Three Years', *Tech iFeng*, 6 May, https://tech.ifeng.com/telecom/special/cmdzs/. Accessed 19 August 2023.

Institute for Chinese Press and Publication (2023). 'The 20th National Reading Survey Report Is Hot Off the press', *China Publishing Today*, 25 April. www.cptoday.cn/news/detail/15353. Accessed 15 October 2023.iReader Tech (2022). 2021 Annual Report of iReader Tech Ltd. Shanghai. http://static.sse.com.cn/disclosure/listedinfo/announcement/c/new/2022-04-23/603533_20220423_25_ZuIvXLsx.pdf.

iReader Tech (2023). *2022 Annual Performance Forecast*. Beijing: iReader Technology Corporation Limited.

iResearch (2018). *Report on Chinese Online Literature Authors*. Beijing: iResearch.

Jenkins, H., Ford, S., & Green, J. (2013). *Spreadable Media: Creating Value and Meaning in a Networked Culture*. New York: NYU Press.

Ji, O. (2023). 'The "Model Dilemma and Inevitability" Behind the Collapse of Yuewen's Performance', *China Economics*, 23 March, http://finance.ce.cn/stock/gsgdbd/202303/23/t20230323_38458933.shtml. Accessed 8 September 2023.

Jia, L., Nieborg, D. B., & Poell, T. (2022). 'On Super Apps and App Stores: Digital Media Logics in China's App Economy', *Media, Culture & Society*, 44(8), pp. 1437–1453. https://doi.org/10.1177/01634437221128937.

Jiang, S. (2019). *In Collaboration with Over 300 Publishing Institutions, The Content Introduction of Yuewen Has Been Comprehensively Upgraded*, 27 December, www.iprchn.com/cipnews/news_content.aspx?newsId=120414. Accessed 23 September 2023.

Jiang, Z. (2018). *Notification on the Cleanup and Rectification of Undesirable Trends in Network Novels, such as Subcultures in Officialdom, by Various Literary Websites*, 27 November, www.thepaper.cn/newsDetail_forward_2677088. Accessed 11 September 2023.

Johnson, M. J. (2021). *Books and Social Media: How the Digital Age Is Shaping the Printed Word*. London: Routledge.

Kenney, M. & Zysman, J. (2020). 'The Platform Economy: Restructuring the Space of Capitalist Accumulation', *Cambridge Journal of Regions, Economy and Society*, 13(1), pp. 55–76. https://doi.org/10.1093/cjres/rsaa001.

Khalid, A. (2023). 'Spotify Gets Serious about Audiobooks', *The Verge*. 3 October, www.theverge.com/2023/10/3/23902039/spotify-audiobooks-subscription-podcast-audible-amazon-pushkin. Accessed 20 October 2023.

Konoval, S. J. (2015). 'Amazon, or the Modern Prometheus: How the Kindle Is Firing Up a Reading Revolution, and Why the Status Quo Is Resisting', *Journal of Law and Commerce*, 33(1), pp. 118–141. https://doi.org/10.5195/JLC.2014.76.

KrASIA Connection (2023). 'Tencent's China Literature Unveils Industry's First Large Language Model for Writers', *KrASIA*, 21 August, https://kr-asia.com/tencents-china-literature-unveils-industrys-first-large-language-model-for-writers. Accessed 19 September 2023.

Kreutzmann-Gallasch, A. & Schroff, S. (2022). 'A Case for Openness – Book Publishing and the Role of Amazon', *IIC – International Review of Intellectual Property and Competition Law*, 53(2), pp. 194–218. https://doi.org/10.1007/s40319-022-01159-w.

Kutzner, K., Petzold, K., & Knackstedt, R. (2019). Characterising Social Reading Platforms: A Taxonomy-Based Approach to Structure the Field. *Wirtschaftsinformatik 2019 Proceedings*. https://aisel.aisnet.org/wi2019/track06/papers/10.

Lei, Y. (2013). 'Amazon's Day One in China: The Role of Amazon's Kindle in China', *Publishing Research Quarterly*, 29(4), pp. 365–370. https://doi.org/10.1007/s12109-013-9334-3.

Li, M. (2017). 'With the Popularity of Apps, Mobile Reading Apps Have Become a Major Hotspot for E-Book Piracy', *Xinhua Net*, 12 April, www.xinhuanet.com/zgjx/2017-04/12/c_136202085.htm. Accessed 18 August 2023.

Li, Q. (2021). 'BTT Battles in Online Literature', *The Paper*, 21 March, www.thepaper.cn/newsDetail_forward_11801941. Accessed 25 August 2023.

Li, X. (2023). 'Farewell, E-Books!', *Zhihu Column*, 28 February, https://zhuanlan.zhihu.com/p/610092303. Accessed 13 August 2023.

Li, Y. (2017). 'China's Tencent Has an Entertainment Reach Hollywood Would Envy', *Wall Street Journal*, 1 June. www.wsj.com/articles/chinas-inescapable-tencent-adds-hollywood-movies-to-its-vast-walled-garden-1496312147. Accessed 13 August 2023.

Li, Y. (2021). 'Free Theory of Network Literature and the Symptoms of Digital Capitalism', *Academic Journal of Zhongzhou*, (296), pp. 153–159.

Liang, K. (2019). 'Agreement Reached in Long-Running Novel Character Dispute', *China Daily*, 10 October, www.chinadaily.com.cn/cndy/2019-10/10/content_37514604.htm. Accessed 11 September 2023.

Liu, B. (2008). 'Use of Digitization to Modernize China's Publishing Industry', *Publishing Research Quarterly*, 24(1), pp. 40–47. https://doi.org/10.1007/s12109-008-9064-0.

Liu, F. (2013). 'Dangdang's Zero-Yuan Promotion Provokes Anger from Publishers, Sparking Controversy Over the Sales Model of E-Book Copyrights'. *Sohu*, 5 July, https://business.sohu.com/20130705/n380746285.shtml. Accessed 21 January 2024.

Liu, J., & Yan, S. (2020, October 3). *Chinese Online Literature Rankings Released, Integrating Stories and Characters into the Zeitgeist*. http://cul.china.com.cn/2020-10/03/content_41317284.htm.

Liu, Y. (2020). 'What Is Going on with WeChat Reading?', *Shenzhen Business News*, 21 May, http://szsb.sznews.com/MB/content/202005/21/content_861880.html. Accessed 23 September 2023.

Liu, Y. (2021). *Dialogue with Cheng Wu, Vice President of Tencent: Creativity Cannot Be Industrialised, but It Can Be Ecologicalized*, 20 June, www.jiemian.com/article/6253680.html. Accessed 12 August 2023.

Loewenstein, A. (2014). 'Kindle v Glass, Apps v Text: The Complicated Future of Books, *The Guardian*, 26 March, www.theguardian.com/commentisfree/2014/mar/26/kindle-v-glass-apps-v-text-the-complicated-future-of-books. Accessed 24 January 2023.

Luo, Y. (2022). 'Illusions of Techno-nationalism', *Journal of International Business Studies*, 53(3), pp. 550–567. https://doi.org/10.1057/s41267-021-00468-5.

Luo, Z. & Li, M. (2022). 'Participatory Censorship: How Online Fandom Community Facilitates Authoritarian Rule', *New Media & Society*, https://doi.org/10.1177/14614448221113923.

Ma, J. (2013). 'Online Book Giveaways Raise Industry Concerns', *China Daily*, 19 April, www.chinadaily.com.cn/life/2013-04/19/content_16422245.htm. Accessed 14 August 2023.

Mansell, R. & Steinmueller, W. E. (2020). *Advanced Introduction to Platform Economics*. Cheltenham, UK: Edward Elgar.

Mei, Y. (2023). *Publication of the '2022 Annual Report on Digital Reading in China: Examining the 225.89 Billion Yuan Subscription Revenue in the Digital Reading Market*, 24 April, www.sohu.com/a/669895152_121123872. Accessed 6 October 2023.

Meng, L. (2019). 'Qidian and Jinjiang Have Successively Suspended Update Sections, Causing a Sharp Drop in Stock Prices for Webnovel Industry Leader', *Yuewen Group*, 27 May, https://m.sohu.com/a/316865479_465270/m.sohu.com/a/316865479_465270. Accessed 11 September 2023.

Meng, Q. (2022). 'Why Kindle Has Become a Product that Cannot Keep Up with the Times?', *China News Weekly*, 9 February, https://new.qq.com/rain/a/20220209A05QZE00. Accessed 13 August 2023.

Meng, S. (2012). 'China's Book Publishing Industry: A Review of 2011', *Publishing Research Quarterly*, 28(2), pp. 124–129. https://doi.org/10.1007/s12109-012-9267-2.

Milliot, J. (2022). 'RELX Remains World's Biggest Book Publisher', *Publishers Weekly*, 7 October, www.publishersweekly.com/pw/by-topic/industry-news/publisher-news/article/90549-global-50-the-world-ranking-of-the-publishing-industry-2021.html. Accessed 3 October 2023.

Montgomery, L., & Priest, E. (2016). Copyright in China's Digital Cultural Industries, in M. Keane (ed.) *Handbook of Cultural and Creative Industries in China*. Cheltenham, UK: Edward Elgar Publishing, pp. 339–359. https://doi.org/10.4337/9781782549864.00036.

Murray, S. (2012). *The Adaptation Industry: The Cultural Economy of Contemporary Literary Adaptation*. London: Routledge.

Mydrivers (2023). *The Tencent QQ Reading Subscription Rules Have Been Changed! They Will No Longer Synchronize with Qidian Subscription Data*, 6 April, https://finance.sina.com.cn/tech/discovery/2023-04-06/doc-imypmcvi2121657.shtml. Accessed 26 September 2023.

Myrberg, C. (2017). 'Why Doesn't Everyone Love Reading E-Books?', *Insights: The UKSG Journal*, 30(3), 115–125. https://doi.org/10.1629/uksg.386.

NetEase Cloud Reading (2016). *2016 Survival Report for Original Online Literature Authors*. www.sohu.com/a/76562265_334205. Accessed 9 September 2023.

Nielsen, R. K. & Sarah, A. G. (2022). *The Power of Platforms*. Oxford, UK: Oxford University Press.

O'Neill, P. H. (2015). 'The Chilling Effect Chinese Censorship Has on Internet-Fiction Authors', *The Daily Dot*, 19 April, www.dailydot.com/debug/chinese-online-fiction-censorship/. Accessed 11 September 2023.

Ong, A. (2006). *Neoliberalism as Exception: Mutations in Citizenship and Sovereignty*. Durham, US: Duke University Press.

Open Book (2023). *The 2022 Annual Report on the Book Retail Market*. Beijing: Open Book.

Ouyang, Y. (2023). 'ChatGPT Is Not the Technical Nemesis of Online Literature Creation', *Arts and Literature Paper*, 24 August, www.zgwypl.com/content/details24_440981.html. Accessed 15 October 2023.

Peng, X. (2023). 'Short Video E-Commerce Emerged as a Highlight in Last Year's Book Retail Market, with the Largest Increase in Book Purchases among Those Born after 2000', *Yi Cai*, 8 January, www.yicai.com/news/101644194.html. Accessed 2 October 2023.

Phillips, A. & Kovač, M. (2022). *Is This a Book?* 1st ed. Cambridge: Cambridge University Press. https://doi.org/10.1017/9781108938389.

Poell, T. & Nieborg, D. & van Dijck, J. (2019). Platformisation. *Internet Policy Review*, 8(4). https://doi.org/10.14763/2019.4.1425.

Potts, J., Hartley, J. D., Montgomery, L., Neylon, C., & Rennie, E. (2017). 'A journal Is a Club: A New Economic Model for Scholarly Publishing', *Prometheus*, 35, pp. 75–92. https://doi.org/10.1080/08109028.2017.1386949.

Qin, A. (2016). 'Craving a Hot TV Show in China? Start Scouring the Web', *The New York Times*, 28 October, www.nytimes.com/2016/10/29/arts/television/craving-a-hot-tv-show-in-china-start-scouring-the-web.html. Accessed 29 August 2023.

Qin, S. (2022). 'Kindle Has Been in China for Nine Years and Has Turned from Prosperity to Decline. Should It Be Said That It Is Useless?', *The Paper*, 24 January, www.thepaper.cn/newsDetail_forward_16417982. Accessed 13 August 2023.